# The Singing

A Selection of West Gallery Music from the Choir Books of
the Parish Church of St. Laurence, Catsfield, Sussex

transcribed and edited by

Edwin Macadam and Tony Singleton

# Contents

## PSALMS

| Page | Title | Metre | First line |
|------|-------|-------|------------|
| 1 | Psalm 8 OV | CM | O God our Lord how wonderful |
| 2 | Psalm 16 OV | CM | I set the Lord still in my sight |
| 3 | Psalm 19 NV | CM | The heav'ns declare thy glory Lord |
| 4 | Psalm 19 NV | CM | The heav'ns declare thy glory Lord |
| 6 | Psalm 23 OV | CM | My shepherd is the living Lord |
| 8 | Psalm 25 OV | SM | I lift my heart to Thee |
| 9 | Psalm 34 NV | CM | Through all the changing scenes of life |
| 10 | Psalm 39 OV | CM | I said I will look to my ways |
| 11 | Psalm 42 NV | CM | As pants the heart for cooling streams |
| 12 | Psalm 43 NV | LM | Just judge of heav'n, against my foes |
| 14 | Psalm 51 NV | SM | Have mercy, Lord, on me |
| 16 | Psalm 61 NV | CM | Lord hear my cry, regard my prayer |
| 17 | Psalm 68 OV | CM | Let God arise and then His foes |
| 18 | Psalm 75 NV | CM | To Thee, O God, we render praise |
| 19 | Psalm 88 NV | LM | To Thee, my God and Saviour |
| 20 | Psalm 90 OV | CM | The Lord has been our sure defence |
| 21 | Psalm 92 Watts | LM | Lord, 'tis a pleasant thing to stand |
| 22 | Psalm 96 OV | CM | Sing ye with praise unto the Lord |
| 24 | Psalm 108 OV | CM | O God, my heart prepared is |
| 26 | Psalm 117 Watts | LM | From all that dwell below the skies |
| 28 | Psalm 128 NV | CM | The man is blest that fears the Lord |

## ANTHEMS

| Page | Title | First line |
|------|-------|------------|
| 30 | A Hymn from Psalm the 150 | O praise the Lord, enthron'd on high |
| 34 | The Dying Christian to his Soul | Vital spark of Heavenly flame |
| 38 | Collect for the 7th after Trinity | Lord of all power and might |
| 41 | From the 52nd Chapter of Isaiah | Awake, awake, put on thy strength |

## HYMNS

| Page | Title | Metre | First line |
|------|-------|-------|------------|
| 46 | Evening Hymn | LM | Glory to Thee, my God, this night |
| 48 | Morning Hymn | LM | Awake my soul and with the sun |
| 49 | Belvidere Hymn | CM | Blest be the dear uniting love |
| 50 | Hymn 165 | CM | Long have I sat beneath the sound |
| 52 | Hymn 428 Rippons | 878787 | O'er the gloomy hills of darkness |
| 54 | Jubilee Hymn | 666688 | Blow ye the trumpets, blow |
| 55 | Advent Hymn | 878787 | Lo he comes with clouds descending |
| 56 | Nativity | 878787 | Hark the herald angels sing |
| 58 | Hymn for Christmas | 4x10 | Christians awake, arise, rejoice and sing |
| 60 | A Funeral Hymn (1) | 666688 | My life's a shade, my days |
| 62 | A Funeral Hymn (2) | CM | Into this world we nothing brought |

CM = 8686      LM = 8888      SM = 6686

# THE CATSFIELD CHOIR BOOKS

In the MacDermott collection of church music, kept in the library of the Sussex Archaeological Society in Barbican House, Lewes, there are nine manuscript books which are thought to have been used by members of the choir of the parish church of St Laurence, Catsfield in East Sussex. The reason for the doubt is that the books have come to the Society from three sources and the records relating to some of the earlier acquisitions are not as detailed as they might be. These sources are Canon MacDermott, Miss Louisa Blackman (grand-daughter of Robert Blackman) and Mr T C Poulter, whose great-grandfather, a Mr Crouch, was a musician in the church band.

| Acc. No | Source | Notes, including size (w=wide; h=high) |
|---|---|---|
| 19926 | Blackman | 24cm w x 14.5cm h, 115 leaves (all music) including 16 detached from Acc. 19927. It contains 79 items when correctly rearranged. The last four leaves are in a later hand. |
| 19927 | Blackman | 24cm w x 14.5cm h, 77 leaves (all music) excluding those in Acc. 19926. Both of these are watermarked 1826, suggesting they were started soon afterwards. It contains 64 items including those in Acc. 19926, 15 of which occur in both books. Many items are in similar hands in both manuscripts. |
| 19690 | Poulter | Three almost identical books, 24cm w x 14.5cm h, clearly copied by the same hand and labelled "Catsfield Choir 1846". Two are watermarked 1834. Each has 88 leaves (51 blank) and contains 33 hymns and psalms. |
| 19691 | Blackman | |
| 19692 | MacDermott | |
| 19693 | Blackman | 31cm w x 23.5cm h and labelled "Catsfield Choir 1840". It has 94 leaves (8 blank) and contains 33 items, mostly anthems but some hymns & psalms. It is not watermarked. |
| 19694 | Poulter | 24.5cm w x 29.5cm h and labelled "Catsfield Choir 1846". It has 78 leaves (22 blank) and contains 20 items, mostly anthems, 6 pieces occurring in Acc. 19693. It is not watermarked. It is in the same hand as Acc. 19690-2. |
| 19895 | MacDermott | Labelled "Catsfield Choir 1850", it contains a distinctly later selection of music, similar to Acc. 19689. Some items are written out in four parts on two staves. |
| 19689 | MacDermott | In a copperplate hand, it is seemingly copied verbatim from a published work. It is entirely in two parts (air and bass) and the quality of the hand suggests that it may have been copied by the Rector's wife for playing on the organ. |

On the evidence of these music books, there was obviously a significant change in the repertoire and the style in which the music was performed in Catsfield church from about 1850 onwards, and consequently only the first seven books listed above have been used as the sources of music for this publication. There is also a printed music book (Acc. 19919) whose musical content is similar to Acc. 19689 entitled *A Selection of the most Approved Psalm & Hymn Tunes arranged by Thomas Henshaw*, with the name of the Rector, Burrell Hayley, written on the title page. Henshaw devoted much of his career to the promotion of the new ideas in parish church music, namely congregational singing led by an organ and a surpliced choir, imitating the cathedral style of performance. The seven books from which this selection is drawn, excluding duplicates, contain 117 psalms, 33 anthems, canticles or set pieces, and 35 hymns, a total of 175 different items of music.

# CANON MACDERMOTT

Canon Kenneth H MacDermott L.Th., A.R.C.M., realised as long ago as the 1890s that not only had a wealth of church music been lost but also that the instruments and the surviving members of the old church bands were fast disappearing. To quote from one of his scrapbooks: "I began my research in the subject of the 'Old Church Gallery Minstrels' in 1895 when I was Curate of Hurstpierpoint, Sussex. An old man named Pierce, aged about 87 at the time, gave me his old manuscript tune book, dated 1829, containing hymn and psalm tunes which had been in use in Hurst church". This is also in the SAS Library (Acc. 19890).

MacDermott was Rector of Selsey, near Chichester in West Sussex, from 1915 to 1925, and then of Buxted in East Sussex from 1925 to 1944. Whilst at Selsey, in 1917, he began a more systematic collection of information by writing to 200 parish church choirmasters throughout Sussex and advertising in the Sussex Gazette, appealing for information about church bands and their music. As a result of these letters and subsequent research he was able to publish an article in *Sussex Archaeological Collections Vol. LX (1919)* and in 1922 he published his first book on the subject, *Sussex Church Music in the Past* (Moore and Wingham, Chichester). This was reprinted in 1923, its publication attracting further correspondence and information from Sussex and beyond, and subsequently in July 1934 MacDermott was invited by the BBC to broadcast on the subject, the programme being entitled "Grandfather's Village Band".

This, in turn, generated more information so that in 1949 he was able to produce a second volume, *The Old Church Gallery Minstrels* (SPCK, London). Just before he died in 1955 he arranged his notes and correspondence into three scrapbooks; the two relating to Sussex he donated to the Sussex Archaeological Society (Acc. 19696-7) of which he was a member, and the third, relating to other counties and which also included correspondence from 1925 to 1945, he donated to the British Library (Add. 47775 A). His collection of manuscripts, printed music books and musical instruments was also left to the Society, although many of the books and instruments from which he drew inspiration were returned to their owners or to the parish churches from which they came. Our researches to date show that many of the instruments have now disappeared, in some instances stolen, and that a number of the manuscripts and printed books have followed their predecessors, which MacDermott tried to save, into oblivion. After his death the Sussex Archaeological Society decided to build on his collection and further volumes of music have either been donated to, or have been purchased by, the Society.

## CATSFIELD AND ITS PARISH CHURCH

The parish of Catsfield covers 2944 acres and the village lies about 5 miles north of Hastings and 2 miles south-west of Battle. The censuses record a population of 589 persons in 1841 and 550 in 1851. It still is a typical rural parish in East Sussex, livestock rather than arable farming being predominant, and with large areas of woodland which in former centuries fuelled several iron bloomeries and furnaces in the area and also provided a variety of types of timber for different rural industries - building construction, fencing and wattles, hop-poles and handtools, and for tanneries and gunpowder making.

The Domesday Book in 1086 mentions the presence of a "little church serving the hall" at Cedesfille, and indeed the core of the nave is late 11th century and contains interesting herringbone masonry of the period. From the censuses and from maps of the time it seems likely that before the 19th century Catsfield had no focal point, it being a number of dispersed settlements and only a handful of dwellings around the Green, now the main village.

The tower was rebuilt in the late 12th century and a number of the chancel windows and the priest's door are 13th century. It was recorded in 1826 that there was a north aisle known as the Ashburnham Chapel "about half the length of the nave ... very narrow and much decayed", but this was renewed when the north aisle was rebuilt and enlarged and the church "restored" in 1847. Thus the main body of the church in the West Gallery period (1700 to 1847) was a single chancel and nave with the tower at its west end and a small north aisle. Late 18th century drawings of the church by James Lambert *(sen)* and S Hieronymus Grimm show a small two-light dormer window in the roof line between the south porch and the tower. This obviously gave light to a gallery, although the only record of this in contemporary writings so far discovered is a single entry in the accounts of a local builder, John Blackman, which he kept between 1800 and 1849. It reads: "Feb 4 1837, Catsfield Church: To mend the sealing *(sic)* and gallery windows". There is now no visible trace in the church of any such construction.

The Rectors during the West Gallery period were:

| | | | |
|---|---|---|---|
| 1708 | Edward Stapley MA | 1810 | William Trivett *(jnr)* MA |
| 1720 | Arthur Coster MA | 1813 | William Delves MA |
| 1750 | Charles Coldcall MA | 1823 | Denny Ashburnham BA |
| 1794 | William Delves MA | 1843 | Burrell Hayley MA |

The Patrons during this time were the Earls of Ashburnham, whose estates included the north-west part of the parish and who had held the living since about 1527, with the exception of the period 1600 to 1687. Denny Ashburnham was the third son of the fifth Baronet and appears simultaneously to have been Vicar of Ditchling.

Burrell Hayley, whose father and grandfather had been Rectors of Brightling (where there is recorded another strong West Gallery band and choir), became Rector in 1843 and, having been educated at Worcester College, Oxford, probably brought with him the latest ideas of the Oxford Movement. He died in 1880, whilst his widow went on to be a centenarian, dying in 1922.

During the West Gallery period it is assumed that the singers and musicians sat, as was usually the case, in the west gallery. Mention is made in correspondence with MacDermott of a long pew at the west end of the church which was referred to as "The Singing Seat" by later generations. This possibly might have been in the gallery itself, and was later transferred to the back of the nave. Almost certainly the gallery was removed when the church was restored in 1847, and in 1850 a "small manual organ placed in the chancel" to accompany the singing. This was played by the Rector's wife, Maria Georgina, who also trained the choir. She was from the Pilkington family who purchased Church House, now known as Catsfield Manor, in the second quarter of the 19th century. Apparently she and her husband lived there with her family in preference to the Rectory, and it was to her drawing room there that the small organ was transferred "when the new and larger instrument was installed in 1883".

## THE MUSIC AND ITS PERFORMERS

West Gallery Music is a generic term now given to music mainly sung in rural and some town parish churches between approximately 1700 and 1850 which was derived from Playford's settings of the Old Version of the metric psalms. Initially each line of the verse was sung by the parish clerk, the pitch being set on a pitch-pipe, and the congregation would follow his "lining out". However, this often resulted in a dirge-like quality to the singing so that reformers encouraged the formation and training of choirs of suitable young people in each parish to lead the congregation in the musical parts of the service. The music quickly evolved during the early part of the 18th century into more ornate fuguing tunes which were less easy for the congregation to join in with and in the latter half of the century the singers were joined by a variety of instruments. Thus the style of music moved from the "old way of singing" with relatively simple block harmonies, to elaborate psalm tunes, services and anthems sung to the accompaniment of the village band, comprising fiddles, bass viol or 'cello, flute, clarinet, hautboy (oboe), bassoon and serpent. It was widely believed to be illegal to sing hymns during a church service until a hearing of a Consistory Court in York in 1820 held otherwise, which paved the way for many collections of hymns to be published.

During this period the singing often became divorced from the congregation and in many places became the sole province of the choir. Moreover, choirs sometimes adopted a rather dictatorial attitude from the west gallery which provoked the ire of many an incumbent and ultimately caused their own downfall. As one of the many radical changes introduced by the Oxford Movement in the mid-19th century the musicians were made redundant, ousted by a simple organ or sometimes even a barrel-organ, as at Brightling, and a reformed choir, often surpliced as in cathedrals, led the congregational singing. The publishing of *Hymns Ancient and Modern* in 1861, in which each hymn was assigned its own particular tune, many written or adapted for congregational singing, was the final death blow to the West Gallery tradition.

We know a little about the Catsfield choir and band at the time although, unfortunately, there are few parish records from the West Gallery period. The churchwardens' accounts have not survived and, apart from the vestry minutes, there is relatively little documentation which might throw light on the choir or its activities. MacDermott corresponded with Herbert Blackman, whose father, Robert, and an uncle (probably James), had both played flutes in the church choir. Robert is recorded as a master builder on a plaque on the Methodist Chapel, which he built in 1912, as was his father, John Blackman who lived between 1773 and 1849. John lived in the area of the Green and was responsible for the building of the village school in the 1840s. Robert and his brother, James, continued in the building trade, both being recorded as bricklayers in the censuses. James was the parish clerk in 1844 and was paid £5 for his services that year. Robert was also intimately involved in parish affairs as his name frequently appears in the vestry minutes, and he was parish constable in 1852. It is likely that several others of the same family were members of the choir and band over this period. MacDermott records that in 1922 a flute used in the church was still in existence.

Some of the music books from the old choir were donated by Mr T C Poulter, whose grandfather was a Mr Crouch, a piccolo player in the band. There were, however, several Crouch families living in Catsfield according to the 1851 census. He might have been Isaac Crouch, then aged 42, an agricultural labourer on parish relief who later served as parish clerk although there were also two other agricultural labourers, Spencer Crouch and William Crouch aged 50 and 55 respectively. It is unlikely to be the latter as it is recorded on a plaque in the entrance to the Methodist

Chapel that William Crouch was one of the "pioneers of Methodism in Catsfield who ... maintained from year to year in this parish amidst many trials and difficulties the teaching of the simple gospel ..." In addition, there was Richard Crouch, aged 56, who was a timber merchant and presumably came from the timber yard at Broomham.

## PRESENTATION OF THE MUSIC

As far as possible what follows is a faithful representation of the music, although some minor editing has been necessary. For example, it often occurs that notes in the manuscript books are indeterminately positioned and can be read as either on the line or in a space. It is also clear that sometimes a note has been incorrectly copied by transposing it by an interval of a third. Where such errors have been detected, the amendment is noted in the music.

It was common practice for the original compilers of manuscript books to omit the bass accompaniment when copying from printed sources, and in the case of 'Psalm 19 NV' by Thomas Clark all the instrumental parts were omitted beyond the notes performed by the singers. The original version is included in this collection along with the manuscript version to show how a piece might be reduced to its basic elements. Considering the labour involved in copying out the music, it is not surprising that bass instrumental lines were omitted because, more often than not, these varied but little from the bass vocal line in simple psalm settings. Variations were sometimes noted in the manuscripts by a doubling at the octave in the bass line or by adding instrumental notes at half-size.

There are many differences in the way music was printed and written between the late 18th century and today. Indeed there were several fundamental changes in music publishing conventions during the century from 1750 to 1850, the period from which this music largely originates. The air or tune was usually in the tenor part and placed above the bass line, as it is today. However, as the ranks of boy trebles were swelled by female singers, they were later allocated the air so that Thomas Clark and some of his contemporaries in the first decades of the 19th century had the treble part printed immediately above the bass, giving a *TASB* assignment of voices. To add to the confusion, by the mid-19th century some publications, including the widely used *Union Tune Book,* used *ASTB* as the assignment of voices. In most cases, however, the parts were written out on four separate staves, the modern convention of setting four voices *SATB* on two staves, and thus separating the sexes, being a typically Victorian invention. In earlier (pre-1800) West Gallery pieces the alto, and sometimes the tenor, parts were set with their own C clefs. This only occurs twice in the Catsfield manuscripts, the example included here being 'Funeral Hymn (1)' in which the alto part has been transcribed into the treble clef.

Since in almost all cases no assignment of voices is given in the manuscript books, the music is presented in the original order. Suggestions have been included in both the music and the index on the inside back cover, and an assignment such as *asTb* indicates that the tenor part has the air or tune. In the manuscripts more often than not *SATB* is satisfactory, but *TASB* may be equally acceptable. A richer sound will result from doubling both male and female voices on the tenor and soprano lines.

In the manuscript books many of the words are often missing, possibly because the musicians would not have needed them, or the singers (many of whom would have been illiterate) knew them, or a copy of the Prayer Book, with the metric psalms at the back, lay beside the manuscript on the music stand in the gallery. Sometimes the verse numbers to be sung are written in the manuscript books but, where words are absent or no indication is given, the policy has been to supply the first four verses unless the original published form from which the music has been traced has other verses printed. One or two suggested doxologies have been added to fit the different metres.

Our final thanks must go to Canon K H MacDermott whose early interest and forethought has preserved this material for us and to members of the West Gallery quire *Sussex Harmony* who have helped us bring much of the music back to life in the last three years.

EDWIN MACADAM     TONY SINGLETON
*Lewes, Sussex*

*July 1995*

# Psalm 8 OV
## (Tune: Otford)

Voices: saTb

(1)
O God our Lord, how wonderful
    Are Thy works everywhere!
Thy fame surmounts in dignity
    The highest heav'ns that are.

(2)
E'en by the mouths of sucking babes
    Thou wilt confound Thy foes;
For in those babes Thy might is seen,
    Thy graces they disclose.

(3)
And when I see the heav'ns above,
    The work of Thine own hand,
The sun, the moon, and all the stars,
    In order as they stand.

(4)
Lord, what is man, that Thou of him,
    Tak'st such abundant care;
Or what the Son of Man, whom Thou
    To visit dost not spare!

The title in the manuscript is 'The 8 Psalm' but no words accompany the music. However, the tune is widely known as 'Otford' and was almost certainly copied from Abraham Adams' *A Psalmist's New Companion*, where it is printed with these words to Psalm 8 OV. The earliest occurrence in print yet found is in *A Collection of 20 New Psalm Tunes Compos'd with a veriety of Fuges after a different manor to any yet Extant Collected Engrav'd and Printed by Mich Beesly, 1746.* Psalm 8 was the proper psalm for Evensong on the second day of the month and for Matins on Ascension Day.    Source: Acc. 19926 p 18

Transcription © Edwin Macadam & Tony Singleton, 1995

# Psalm 16 OV

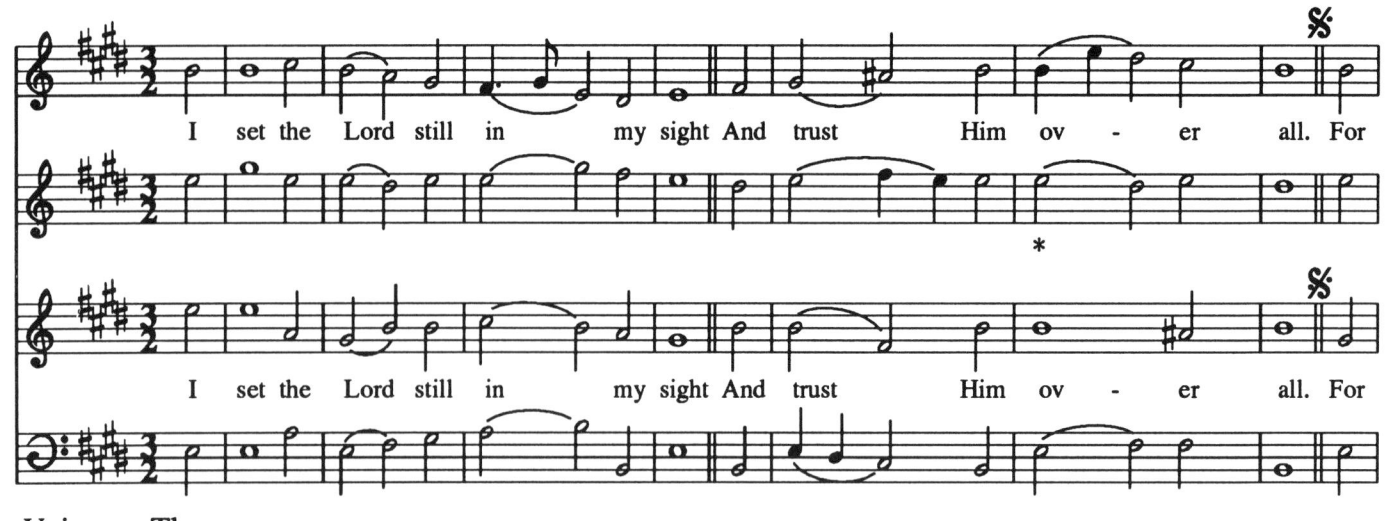

Voices: saTb

(8)
I set the Lord still in my sight
 And trust Him over all,
For He doth stand on my right hand
 Therefore I shall not fall.

(9)
Wherefore my heart and tongue also
 Rejoice exceedingly,
My flesh likewise doth rest on hope
 To rise again; for why?

(10)
Thou wilt not leave my soul in hell
 Because Thou lovest me,
Nor yet wilt give Thy Holy One
 Corruption for to see.

(11)
But wilt me shew the way to life
 Where there is joy in store,
And where at Thy right hand there are
 Pleasures for evermore.

Psalm 16 is the proper psalm for the morning service on the third day of the month.
Source: Acc. 19927 p 32          * bar 7: C in ms

Transcription © Edwin Macadam & Tony Singleton, 1995

# The Singing Seat

# Psalm 19 NV

Voices: taSb

The heav'ns declare Thy glory Lord

The heav'ns declare Thy glo - - ry, Lord Which Thou a-

The heav'ns declare Thy glory Lord Which Thou a-

The firmament and stars express

lone canst fill — Their great Cre-a-tor's

The firmament and stars express

lone canst fill — Their

Their great Cre-a-tor's skill. Their great Cre-a-tor's skill. skill.

skill. Their great Cre-a-tor's skill. Their great Cre - a - tor's skill. skill.

Their great Cre-a-tor's skill. Their great Cre - a - tor's skill. skill.

great Cre-a-tor's skill. Their great Cre-a-tor's skill. Their great Cre-a-tor's skill. skill.

Psalm 19 NV comes from Thomas Clark's *A Set of Psalm Tunes* (the first of many). The original is given overleaf for comparison and illustrates how the instrumental sections have been pruned down. The doubling of notes in the bass line above suggests what a 'cello or bassoon might have played at Catsfield. However, these extra bass notes only occur in Acc. 19927.      Source: Acc. 19926 p 45 & 19927 p

Transcription © Edwin Macadam & Tony Singleton, 1995

# Psalm 19 NV

# The Singing Seat
### Errata and Addenda

| | | |
|---|---|---|
| IFC | | Bottom line: "and desktop printed in "Ovation" on an Acorn A5000" |
| 1 | Psalm 8 OV | Bar 1, alto line: crotchet C should be C sharp |
| 2 | Psalm 16 OV | Air in top line: Satb |
| 3 | Psalm 19 NV | Bar 4, alto line: minim F should be G; |
| | | Bar 6, semi-quaver D should be E; |
| | | bottom line "Source" should end: "19927 p. 34" |
| 4 | Psalm 19 NV | Bar 24, alto line: quaver E should be semi-quaver |
| 7 | Psalm 23 OV | Bar 35, alto line: crotchet E should be D |
| 8 | Psalm 25 OV | Voices: saTb. By William Arnold of Portsea, 1807 |
| 11 | Psalm 42 NV | Bar 16, tenor line: minim D should be C. The tune is 'Axbridge' by Thomas Clark, and published in *A First Set of Psalm Tunes*, with minor emendations, and with voices taSb |
| 12 | Psalm 43 NV | An additional piece in the 2nd edition of William Burgiss 1808 book *Eight Anthems, Twelve Psalms, etc.* |
| 13 | Psalm 43 NV | Composed by William H Burgiss of Heckfield, Hants, in his *Eight Anthems, Twelve Psalm Tunes and Gloria Patri . . . Adapted for the Use of Country Choirs*, London 1808. |
| 16 | Psalm 61 NV | suggested editing: |
| | | Bar 21, alto line: minim G to be F; |
| | | Bars 26 - 27, soprano line: minim A to be B |
| | | Probably by William Figg, 1802 |
| 19 | Psalm 88 NV | Known variously as 'Leominster', 'Clare', 'Berwick', and 'Wells' (in 1750). Earliest reference to this tune is in Israel Holdroyd's *The Spiritual Man's Companion*, 1722 |
| 20 | Psalm 90 OV | 'Bognor' was published in *Harmonia Sacra Londiniensis* by Thomas Purday 1806-07 |
| 22 | Psalm 96 OV | Bar 9, alto line: semibreve E should be C; |
| | | Bar 16, alto line: crotchet D should be F |
| 24 | Psalm 108 OV | Earliest known printing 1760 |
| 25 | Psalm 108 OV | Bar 19, soprano line: notes should be CCEE |
| 26 | Para of Ps 117 | From Thomas Williams' *Psalmodia Evangelica*, 1789, called 'Lea'. |
| 28 | Osalm 128 NV | Called' Hythe', by William Marsh, 1816 |
| 30 | A Hymn 150 | Voices: satb (no one dominant part); |
| | | Bar 43, soprano line: crotchet C should be G; |
| | | Bar 44, soprano line: semibreve A should be D; |
| | | Bar 45, tenor line: crotchet B should be A; also bass, crotchet B should be A |
| 36 | The Dying C | Bar 74: the quaver rest is editorial |
| 42 | An Anthem | Bar 21, bass line: rest should be a crotchet B; |
| | | Bars 47 - 48, soprano line: three Cs should be As |
| | | Bars 56 - 58, "Break forth with joy", soprano line: should be ABBBB; |
| | | Bar 63, alto line: EE should be GG |
| | | Bar 83, tenor line and last bar alto line: appoggiaturas omitted; |
| | | Editorial notes: * Bar 16 should read Bar 15; |
| 49 | Belvidere | Probably by G Titler, 1812 |
| 53 | Hymn 428 | Accompanying notes should read: " ... being published in his *An Eighth Set of Psalms* and with voices taSb." |
| 54 | Jubilee Hymn | The tune is 'Dunstable' by Thomas Clark, published in *A First Set of Psalm and Hymn Tunes*, with minor emendations, and with voices taSb |
| 55 | Advent Hymn | Voices: asTb (also error on IBC). First published by Samuel Webbe, Snr., 1782. |
| 56 | Nativity | by Charles Burney, 1769. |
| 58 | Hymn for Chr | Bar 3, bass line: crotchet G should be F |
| 60 | Funeral Hymn 1 | *New Church Melody*, by William Knapp, 1751 |
| 62 | Funeral Hymn 2 | William Tansu'r, *Collection of Psalm Tunes*, 1711. Once only to these words, 1772. |
| IBC | Psalm 88 | Time signature should be the reversed C |

AFS / ELM November 2000, rev. Mar 2007.

New address for Sussex Harmony Publications:
30 Eynsham Road, Botley, OXFORD. OX2 9BP Tel: 01865 - 865773

(1)
The heav'ns declare Thy glory Lord
    Which Thou alone canst fill.
The firmament and stars express
    Their great Creator's skill.

(2)
The dawn of each returning day
    Fresh beams of knowledge brings;
And from the dark returns of night
    Divine instruction springs.

(3)
Their pow'rful language to no realm
    Or region is confin'd.
'Tis nature's voice, and understood
    Alike by all mankind.

(4)
Their doctrine does its sacred sense
    Through earth's extent display;
Whose bright contents the circling sun
    Does round the world convey.

Transcription © Edwin Macadam & Tony Singleton, 1995

# Psalm 23 OV

*Sym*

Voices: taSb

My shep-herd is, My shep-herd is the li - ving Lord, No-thing there-fore I

My shep-herd is the li - ving Lord, No-thing there-fore I

My shep-herd is, My shep-herd is the li - ving Lord, No-thing there-fore I

My shep-herd is the li - ving Lord, No-thing there-fore I

need. *For* He

need. *Pia* In pa-stures fair near plea - sant streams He

need. *Sym* *For* He

need. *Pia* In pa-stures fair near plea - sant streams He

Transcription © Edwin Macadam & Tony Singleton, 1995

(1)
My shepherd is the living Lord
  Nothing therefore I need
In pastures fair, near pleasant streams
  He setteth me to feed.

(2)
He shall convert and glad my soul,
  And bring my mind in frame,
To walk in paths of righteousness,
  For His most Holy Name.

(3)
Yea, tho' I walk in vale of death,
  Yet will I fear no ill,
Thy rod and staff do comfort me,
  And Thou art with me still

(4)
And in the presence of my foes,
  My table thou shalt spread
Thou wilt fill full my cup, and Thou
  Anointed hath my head.

This version of Psalm 23 OV also comes from Thomas Clark's *A Set of Psalm Tunes with Symphonies and an Instrumental Bass Adapted for the use of Parochial or Country Choirs*, published in 1804, where the voices are assigned *TASB* with the sopranos/trebles singing the air on the third line. However, in the ms copy, transcribed here, the assignment of voices and the bass accompaniment are omitted. Psalm 23 was the proper psalm for the evening service on the fourth day of the month and also for Whitsunday.
Source: Acc. 19926 p 62

Transcription © Edwin Macadam & Tony Singleton, 1995

# Psalm 25 OV
## Tune: Sarah

Voices: asTb

(1)
I lift my heart to Thee
    My God and guide most just
Now suffer me to take no shame
    For in Thee I do trust.

(2)
Let not my foes rejoice
    Nor make no scorn of me
And let them not be ever thrown
    That put their trust in Thee.

(9)
The humble He will teach
    His precepts to obey
He will direct in all His paths
    The lowly man alway.

(10)
For all the ways of God
    Both truth and mercy are
To them that do His covenant
    And statutes keep with care.

The tune comes right at the end of the 1846 ms books with these verses but the tune appears under the heading Sarah in an earlier ms book, again at the back and written in a much later hand than the rest of the book, which rather suggests that all these books were used concurrently.

Presumably the doubling of notes in the later bars of the bass line indicates the notes played by a 'cello or bassoon accompaniment. The psalm is proper for morning service on the fifth day of the month.

Source: Acc. 19690-2 p 3 and 19926 p 91

Transcription © Edwin Macadam & Tony Singleton, 1995

# Psalm 34 NV

Voices: asTb

(2)
Of His deliv'rance I will boast
Till all that are distrest
From my example comfort take
And charm their griefs to rest.

(3)
O magnify the Lord with me,
With me exalt His Name
When in distress to Him I call'd,
He to my rescue came.

(4)
Their drooping hearts were soon refresh'd
Who look'd to Him for aid
Desir'd success in ev'ry face
A cheerful air display'd.

Source: Acc. 19927 p 77 (the second page has been stuck in later in the book)

Transcription © Edwin Macadam & Tony Singleton, 1995

# Psalm 39 OV

Voices: saTb

*(5)*
Lord number out my life and days
    Which yet I have not past,
So that I may be certified,
    How long my life shall last.

*(6)*
For Thou hast pointed out my life
    In length much like a span.
My age is nothing unto me,
    So vain is ev'ry man.

*(14)*
O spare a little, give me space
    My strength for to restore,
Before I go away from hence
    And shall be seen no more.

In the Prayer Book, Psalm 39 is part of the funeral service.    Source: Acc. 19926 p 5 and 19927 p 19.

Transcription © Edwin Macadam & Tony Singleton, 1995

# Psalm 42 NV

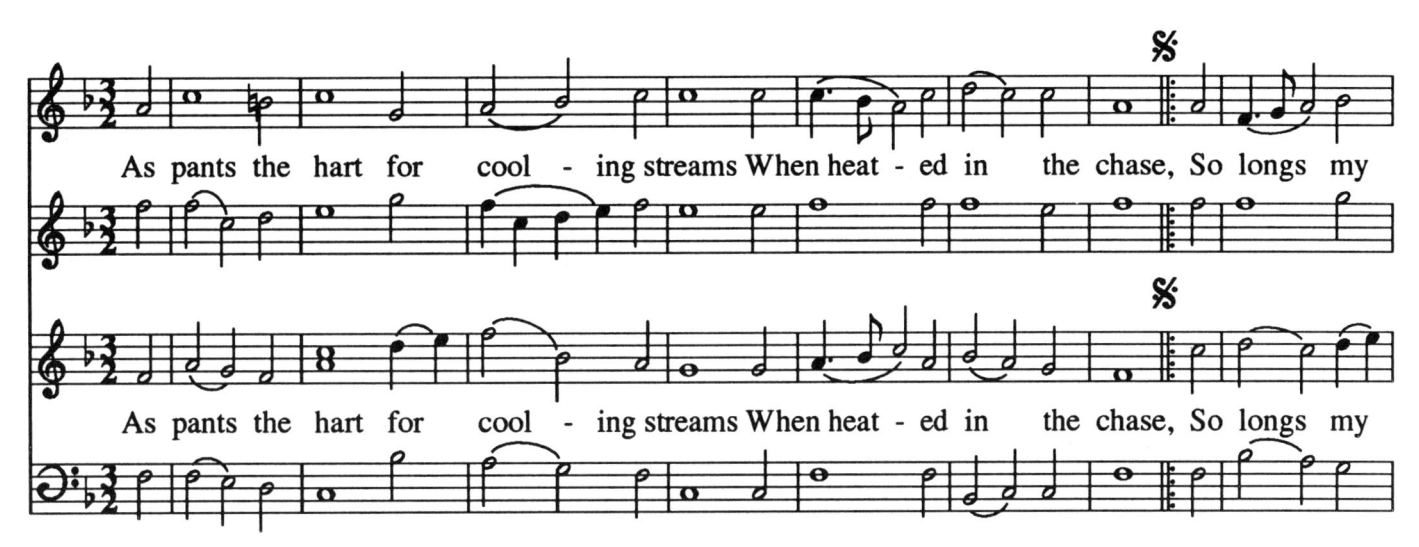

Voices: saTb

(1)
As pants the hart for cooling streams
When heated in the chase,
So longs my soul, O God, for Thee
And thy refreshing grace.

(2)
For Thee, my God, the living God,
My thirsty soul doth pine
O when shall I behold Thy face
Thou Majesty divine?

(4)
I sigh whene'er my musing thoughts
Those happy days present
When I with troops of pious friends
Thy temple did frequent.

(11)
Why restless, why cast down my soul?
Hope still and thou shalt sing
The praise of him who is thy God
Thy health's eternal spring.

Psalm 42 is the proper psalm for the Thursday before Easter and for the evening service on the eighth day of the month.
Source: Acc. 19927 p 54

Transcription © Edwin Macadam & Tony Singleton, 1995

# Psalm 43 NV

Voices: saTb

## The Singing Seat

(1)
Just judge of heav'n, against my foes,
    Do Thou assert my injur'd right
O set me free, my God, from those
    Who in deceit and wrong delight.

(2)
Since Thou art still my only stay,
    Why leav'st Thou me in deep distress?
Why go I mourning all the day,
    Whilst me insulting foes oppress?

(3)
Let me with light and truth be bless'd,
    Be these my guides and lead the way,
Till on Thy holy hill I rest,
    And in Thy sacred temple pray.

(4)
Then will I there fresh altars raise
    To God, who is my only joy;
And well-tun'd harps, with songs of praise
    Shall all my grateful hours employ.

(5)
Why then cast down, my soul? And why
    So much oppress'd with anxious care?
On God, thy God, for aid rely,
    Who will thy ruin'd state repair.

Doxology
To Father, Son and Holy Ghost
    The God whom earth and heav'n adore,
Be glory as it was of old,
    Is now and shall be evermore.

This setting of Psalm 43 NV must have been popular over a period in Catsfield church as it appears in one of the early books and at the end of a book dated 1846. Verse 5 and the doxology have been added here for completeness.

Psalm 43 was the proper psalm for the evening service on the eighth day of the month.

Sources: Acc. 19927 p 46 and 19690-2 p 32

Transcription © Edwin Macadam & Tony Singleton, 1995

# Psalm 51 NV

Voices: saTb or taSb

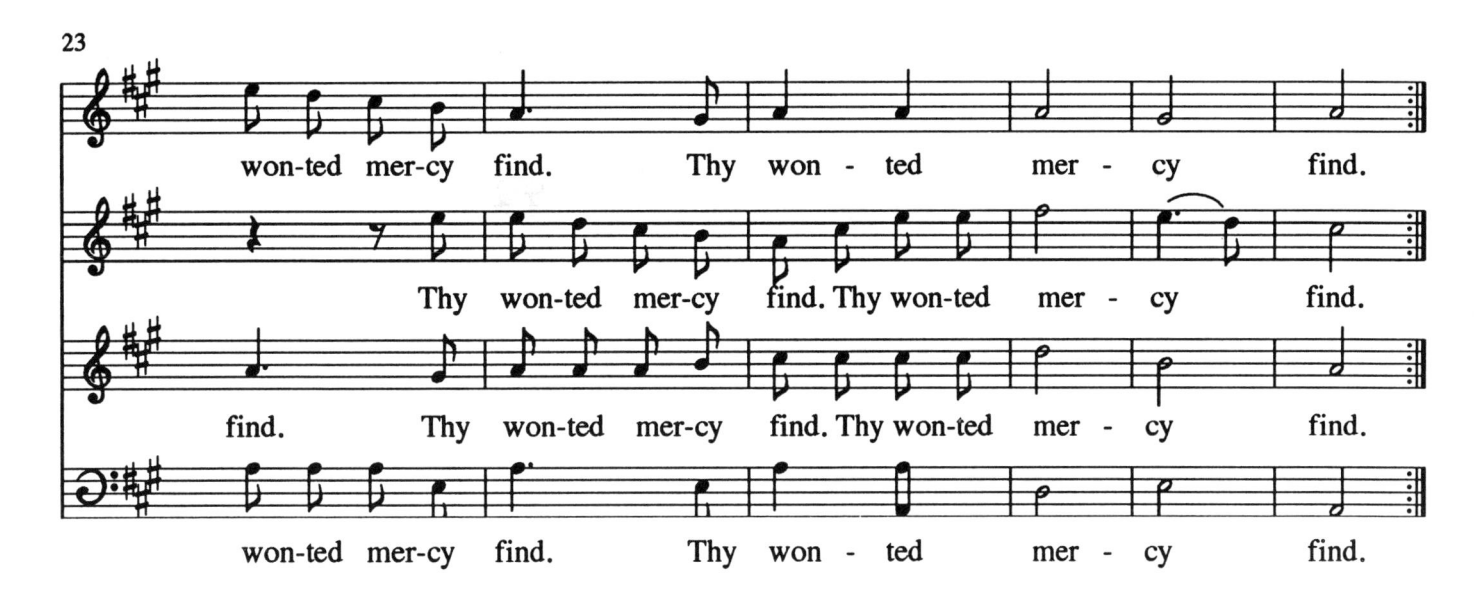

(1)
Have mercy, Lord, on me,
　　As Thou wert ever kind:
Let me, opprest with loads of guilt,
　　Thy wonted mercy find.

(2)
Wash off my foul offence
　　And cleanse me from my sin:
For I confess my crime and see
　　How great my guilt has been.

(4)
Against Thee, Lord, alone,
　　And only in Thy sight,
Have I transgress'd, and, though condemn'd,
　　Must own Thy judgement right.

(6)
Bless Thou, whose searching eye
　　Doth inward truth require.
In secret didst with wisdom's law
　　My tender soul inspire.

This psalm appears in an earlier manuscript book with the air/melody in the top line. However, this version is taken from a later book, dated 1846, where the air is in the third line. Unusually, all the words are written out with the music in both manuscript sources.

Psalm 51 was the proper psalm for the first day in Lent.

Sources: Acc. 19927 p 52 and 19690-2 p 4

Transcription © Edwin Macadam & Tony Singleton, 1995

# Psalm 61 NV

(1)
Lord hear my cry, regard my prayer
Which I, oppress'd with grief,
From earth's remotest parts address,
To Thee for kind relief.

(2/3)
O lodge me safe beyond the reach
Of persecuting power;
Thou who so oft from spiteful foes
Hast been my shelt'ring tower.

(8)
So shall I ever sing Thy praise,
Thy name forever bless;
Devote my prosp'rous days to pay
The vows of my distress.

Psalm 61 is proper for evening service on the eleventh day of the month.

Source: Acc. 19690-2 p 16

Transcription © Edwin Macadam & Tony Singleton, 1995

# Psalm 68 OV

Voices: saTb

(1)
Let God arise and then his foes
　　Will turn themselves to fight.
His enemies for fear shall run
　　And scatter out of sight.

(2)
And as wax melts before the fire
　　And wind blows smoke away,
So in the presence of the Lord
　　The wicked shall decay.

(3)
But righteous men before the Lord
　　Shall heartily rejoice.
They shall be glad and merry all
　　And cheerful in their voice.

(4)
Sing praise, sing praise unto the Lord
　　Who rideth on the sky.
Extol the great Jehovah's name
　　And Him still magnify.

Psalm 68 was the proper psalm for morning service on the thirteenth day of the month and also on Ascension Day and Whitsunday.

Source: Acc. 19926 p 57

Transcription © Edwin Macadam & Tony Singleton, 1995

# Psalm 75 NV

## Tune: Lansdown

Voices: saTb

(2/3)
In Israel when my throne is fix'd,
With me shall justice reign:
The land with discord shakes, but I
The sinking frame sustain.

(4)
Deluded wretches I advis'd
Their errors to redress,
And warn' bold sinners that they should
Their swelling pride suppress.

(5)
Bear not yourself so high, as if
No pow'r could yours restrain:
Submit your stubborn necks, and learn
To speak with less disdain.

Transcription © Edwin Macadam & Tony Singleton, 1995

# Psalm 88 NV

Voices: saTb

(1/2)
To Thee, my God and Saviour, I
  By day and night address my cry;
Vouchsafe my mournful voice to hear,
  To my distress incline Thine ear.

(3/4)
For seas of trouble me invade,
  My soul draws nigh to death's cold shade;
Like one who's strength and hopes are fled
  They number me among the dead.

(5/6)
Like those, who shrouded in the grave,
  From Thee no more remembrance have
Cast off from Thy sustaining care;
  Down to the confines of despair.

(7)
Thy wrath has hard upon me lain,
  Afflicting me with restless pain;
Me all Thy mountain waves have prest,
  Too weak, alas! to bear the least.

This psalm was proper for the Tuesday before Easter and for evening service on Good Friday. It was also prescribed for the morning service on the seventeenth day of the month. This psalm with the same tune occurs in two other ms books in the MacDermott collection, although with different harmonisations.
Source: Acc. 19926 p 40 and 19927 p 38         * last bar: the tenor chord is D/F in ms.

❖❖❖❖❖❖❖❖❖❖❖❖❖❖

**Lansdown** (opposite) was published in W J White's *New Sacred Melodies* and may have been composed by him. The seventh edition was published c.1825.   Source: Acc. 19690-2 p 21

Transcription © Edwin Macadam & Tony Singleton, 1995

# Psalm 90 OV — Tune: Bognor

Voices: saTb

(1)
Thou, Lord, hast been our sure defence,
  Our place of ease and rest,
In all times past, yea, so long since
  As cannot be express'd.

(3)
Thou grindest man through grief and pain
  To dust or clay, and then,
Thou unto them dost say again,
  Return ye sons of men.

(4)
The lasting of a thousand years,
  What is it in thy sight?
As yesterday it doth appear,
  Or as a watch by night.

(10)
The time of our abode on earth
  Is threescore years and ten;
But if we come to fourscore years,
  Our life is grievous then.

The composer is given in the ms book as J. Waters, of whom nothing is known, although it is tempting to suggest that he may be a Sussex man, as the tune has been given a Sussex title. Psalm 90 OV is an alternative to Psalm 39 for the funeral service and is also suggested in some printed psalmodies for services on the 30th January to commemorate the "Martyrdom of the Blessed King Charles the First". The psalm is divided into two parts, the first part contains verses of a rather depressing nature, typified by those above, but the second part has a more positive and joyful feel to the verses.

Source: Acc. 19690-2 p 25

Transcription © Edwin Macadam & Tony Singleton, 1995

# Psalm 92 Dr Watts

Lord 'tis a pleas-ant thing to stand In gar-dens plant-ed by Thy hand *Sym*

Lord 'tis a pleas-ant thing to stand In gar-dens plant-ed by Thy hand *Sym*

Voices: taSb

Let me with-in thy courts be seen — *Forte* Like a young ce-dar

Let me with-in thy courts be seen *Pia* — *Pia* *Forte* Like a young ce-dar, Like a young ce-dar

Like a young ce-dar — Like a young cedar

fresh and green *Sym*

fresh and green *Sym*

(2)
There grow thy saints in faith and love
    Blest with thine influence from above
Not Lebanon with all its trees
    Yields such a comely sight as these.

(3)
The plants of grace shall ever live
    Nature decays but grace must thrive
Time that doth all things else impair
    Still makes them flourish strong and fair.

(4)
Laden with fruits of age, they show
    The Lord is holy, just and true
None that attend his gates shall find
    A God unfaithful or unkind.

This is taken substantially from acc. 19927 p 4, where it appears with these words by Isaac Watts. In acc. 19926 p 11 it is written out in the key of A major without any of the instrumental symphonies. The tune was composed by Thomas Clark and published with these words set to it in his *A Third Set of Psalm Tunes* where it was in A major and originally had an opening symphony and instrumental bass. The tune is entitled 'Cedar' in a ms book compiled by John Moore of Wellington in Shropshire.

Transcription © Edwin Macadam & Tony Singleton, 1995

# Psalm 96 OV
## (Tune: Pentonville)

Sing ye with praise un-to the Lord New songs with joy and mirth, New songs with joy and mirth; Sing un-to him with one ac-cord, All peo-ple on the earth All peo-ple on the earth All peo-ple on the earth All peo-ple on the

Voices: saTb

Transcription © Edwin Macadam & Tony Singleton, 1995

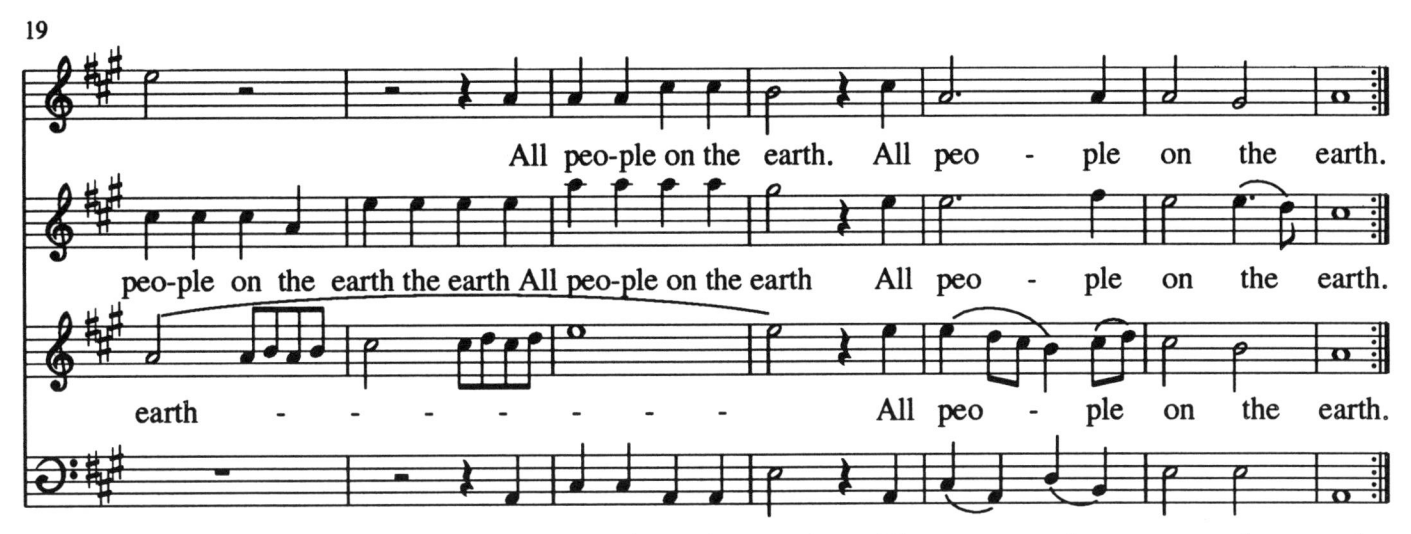

## The Singing Seat

*[Musical notation with four vocal parts, measure 19, with lyrics:]*

*Soprano:* All peo-ple on the earth. All peo - ple on the earth.

*Alto:* peo-ple on the earth the earth All peo-ple on the earth All peo - ple on the earth.

*Tenor:* earth - - - - - - All peo - ple on the earth.

*Bass:* All peo-ple on the earth. All peo - ple on the earth.

(1)
Sing ye with praise unto the Lord
    New songs with joy and mirth;
Sing unto him with one accord,
    All people on the earth.

(2)
Yea sing unto the Lord alway,
    Praise ye his holy name;
Declare and shew from day to day
    Salvation by the same.

(3)
Among the heathens all declare
    His honour round about;
To shew his wonders do not spare
    In all the world throughout.

(4)
For why? The Lord is great in might,
    And worthy of all praise;
And he is to be fear'd of right
    Above all gods always.

Doxology
To Father, Son, and Holy Ghost,
    The God whom we adore,
Be glory; as it was, is now,
    And shall be evermore.

This tune was quite popular and was published in many collections including, relatively locally, *A Set of New Psalm & Hymn Tunes* by William Marsh of Canterbury,

Psalm 96 is the proper psalm for the morning service on the nineteenth day of the month and for the Sunday after Ascension day.

Source: Acc. 19926 p 88 and 19690-2 p 8

The font in Catsfield church

Transcription © Edwin Macadam & Tony Singleton, 1995

# Psalm 108 OV
## (Tune: Milford)

Voices: saTb

Transcription © Edwin Macadam & Tony Singleton, 1995

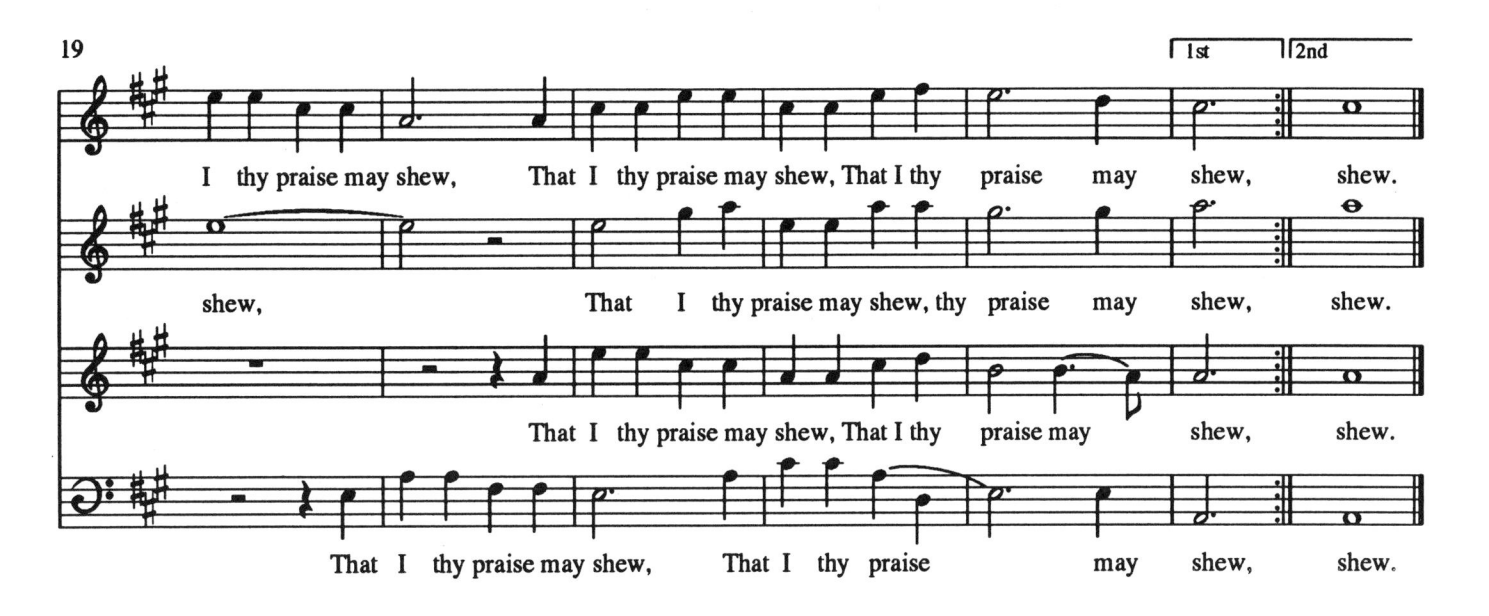

(1)
O God, my heart prepared is,
    My tongue is likewise so;
I will advance my voice in song,
    That I thy praise may shew.

(2)
Awake, my viol and my harp,
    Sweet melody to make,
And in the morning I myself
    Right early will awake.

(3)
By me among the people, Lord,
    Still praised shalt thou be:
And I among the heathen folk
    Will praises sing to Thee.

(4)
Because the mercy doth ascend
    Above the heavens high:
Also Thy truth doth reach the clouds
    Within the lofty sky.

This tune is 'Milford' by Joseph Stephenson (1723 - 1810), clerk of the Unitarian Chapel in Poole for a substantial period in the latter half of the eighteenth century, and who was a prolific composer and publisher of sacred music, particularly in the fuguing style, as illustrated here.

Psalm 108 was the proper psalm for the evening service on Ascension Day as well as on the 22nd day of the month.

Source: Acc. 19926 p 71 and 19927 p 51; the first and second time bars have been added.

Transcription © Edwin Macadam & Tony Singleton, 1995

# Paraphrase of Psalm 117

Voices: sTb

Transcription © Edwin Macadam & Tony Singleton, 1995

(3)
Your lofty themes, ye mortals, bring;
In songs of praise divinely sing;
The great salvation loud proclaim,
And shout for joy the Saviour's name.

(4)
Praise God, from whom all blessings flow;
Praise Him, all creatures here below;
Praise Him above, ye heavenly host;
Praise Father, Son, and Holy Ghost.

This piece appears with the above title although the words are actually verses 1 & 2 of Isaac Watts' version of Psalm 117. It also appears as no. 699 in *Wesley's Hymns* from whence verses 3 & 4 are supplied, although it is possible that this piece was written as a short anthem. Psalm 117 is the proper psalm for the twenty fourth day of the month.

Source: Acc. 19927 p 62     * bar17: C in ms

# Psalm 128 NV

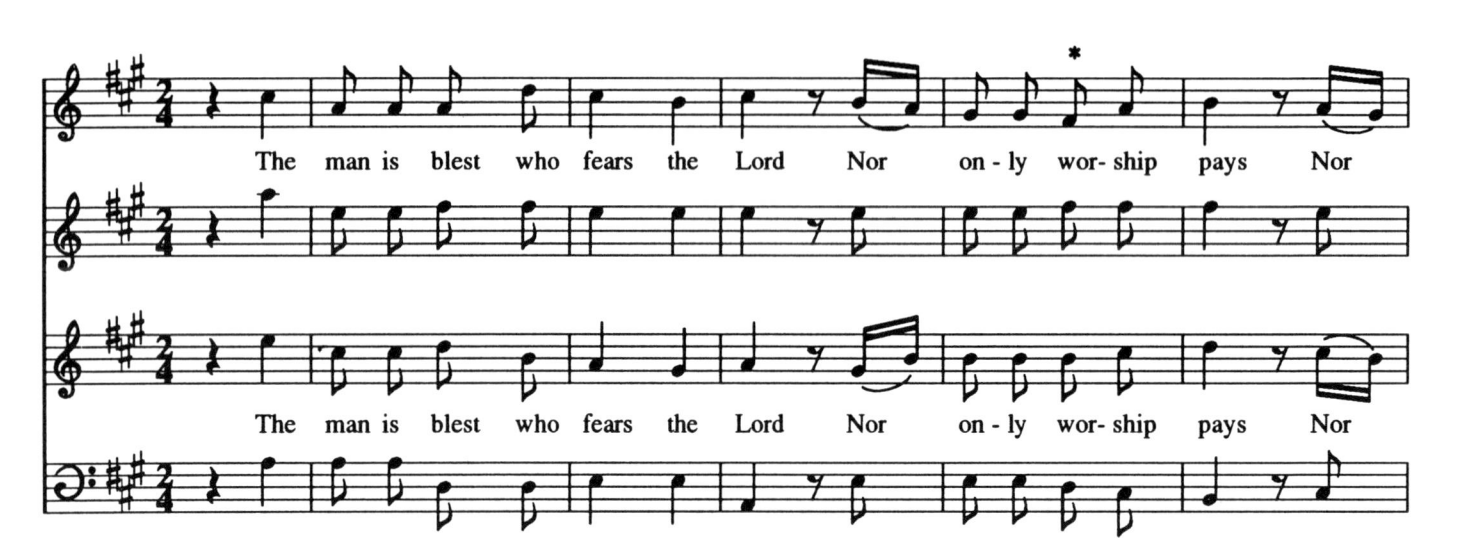

Voices: saTb

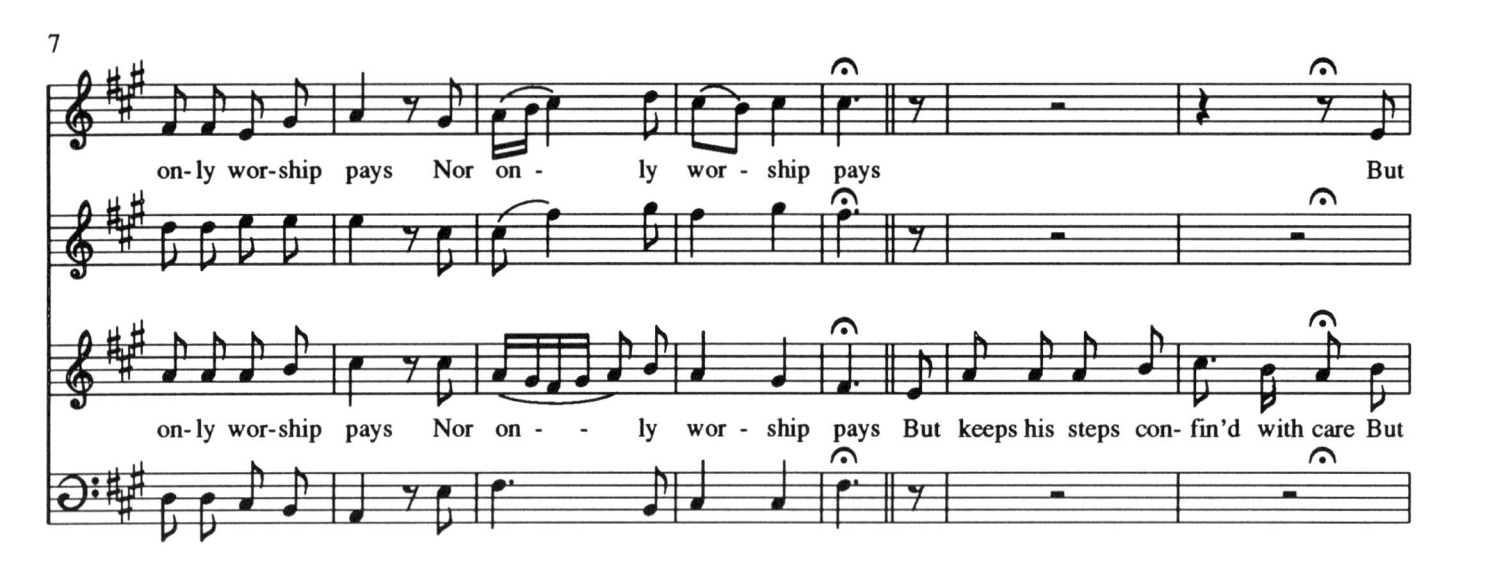

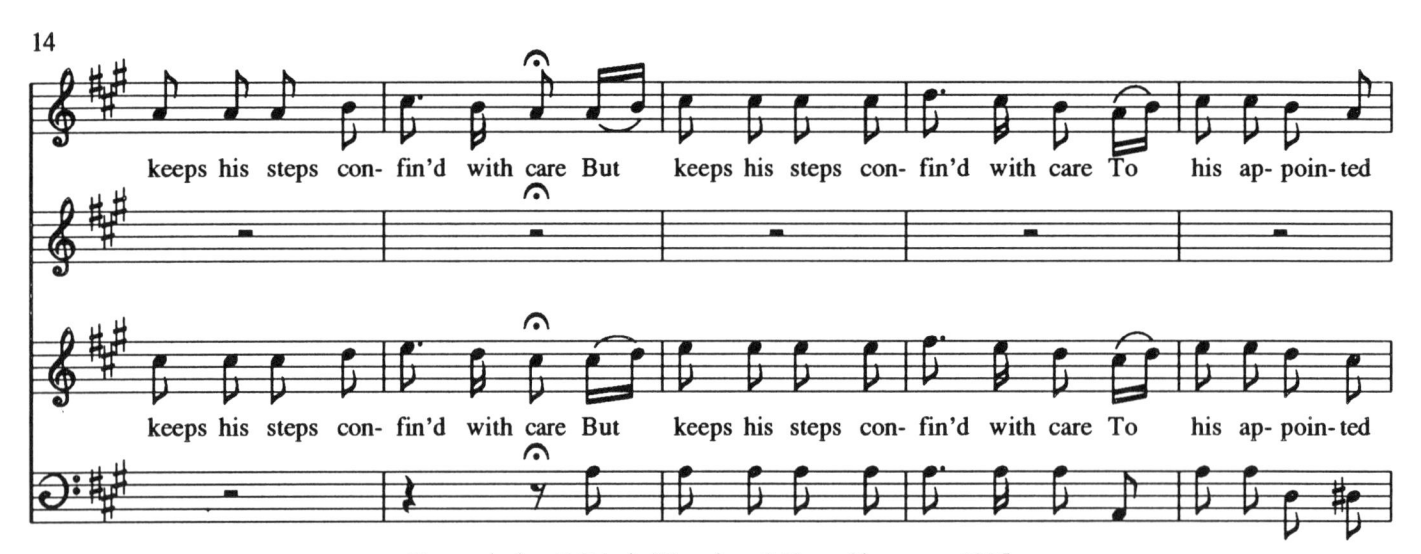

Transcription © Edwin Macadam & Tony Singleton, 1995

## (1)
The man is blest who fears the Lord
 Nor only worship pays
 But keeps his steps confin'd with care
 To his appointed ways.

## (2)
He shall upon the sweet returns
 Of his own labours feed
 Without dependence live and see
 His wishes all succeed.

## (3)
His wife like a fair fertile vine
 Her lovely fruit shall bring
 His children like young olive plants
 About his table spring.

## (4/5)
Who fears the Lord shall prosper thus;
 Him Sion's God shall bless,
 And grant him all his days to see
 Jerusalem's success.

## (6)
He shall live on till heirs from him
 Descend with vast increase,
 Much bless'd in his own prosp'rous state
 And more in Israel's peace.

In the ms book verses 1, 2, 3 and 6 are written out with the music. Verse 4/5 has been added as it completes this short psalm which is prescribed in the Prayer Book for use during the evening service on the 27th day of the month. The psalm was also a favourite to be said or sung during the Wedding Service after the blessing which followed the pronouncement of the couple as man and wife. Clearly verse 3 influenced the choice of psalm for this occasion.

Source: Acc. 19927 p 10
* bar 5: G in ms

Transcription © Edwin Macadam & Tony Singleton, 1995

# A Hymn from Psalm the 150

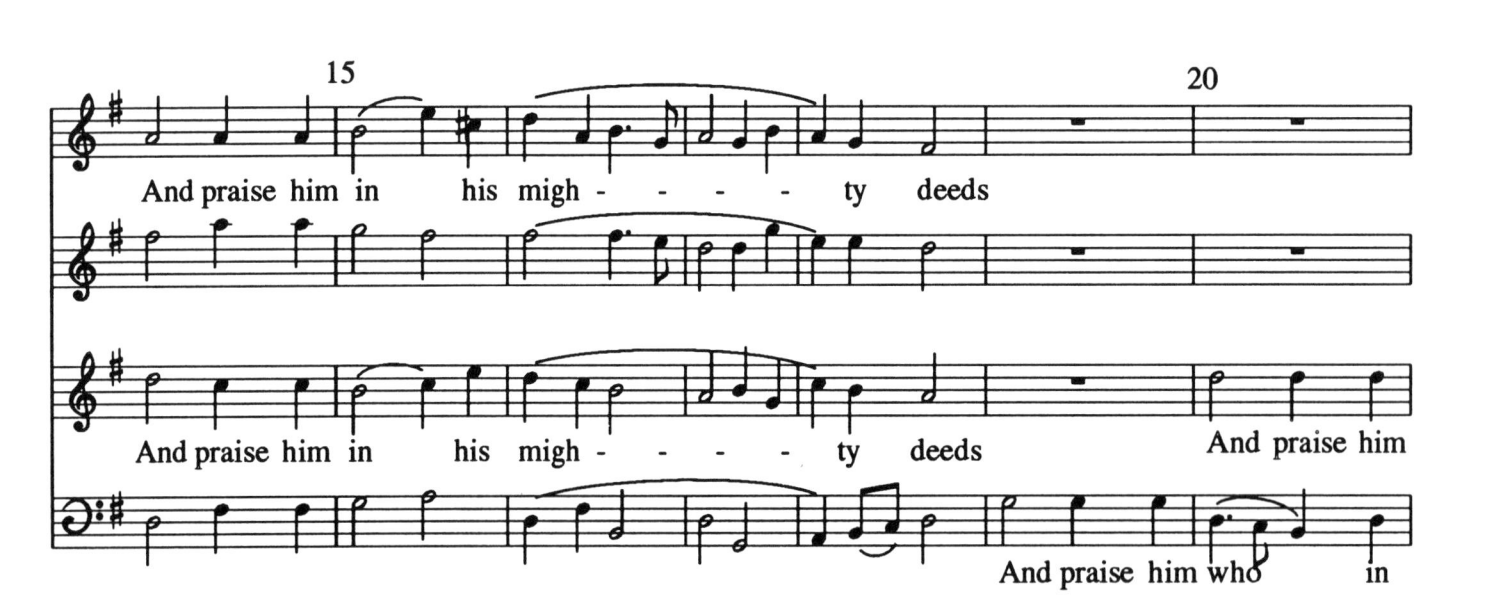

Voices: astb

Transcription © Edwin Macadam & Tony Singleton, 1995

# The Singing Seat

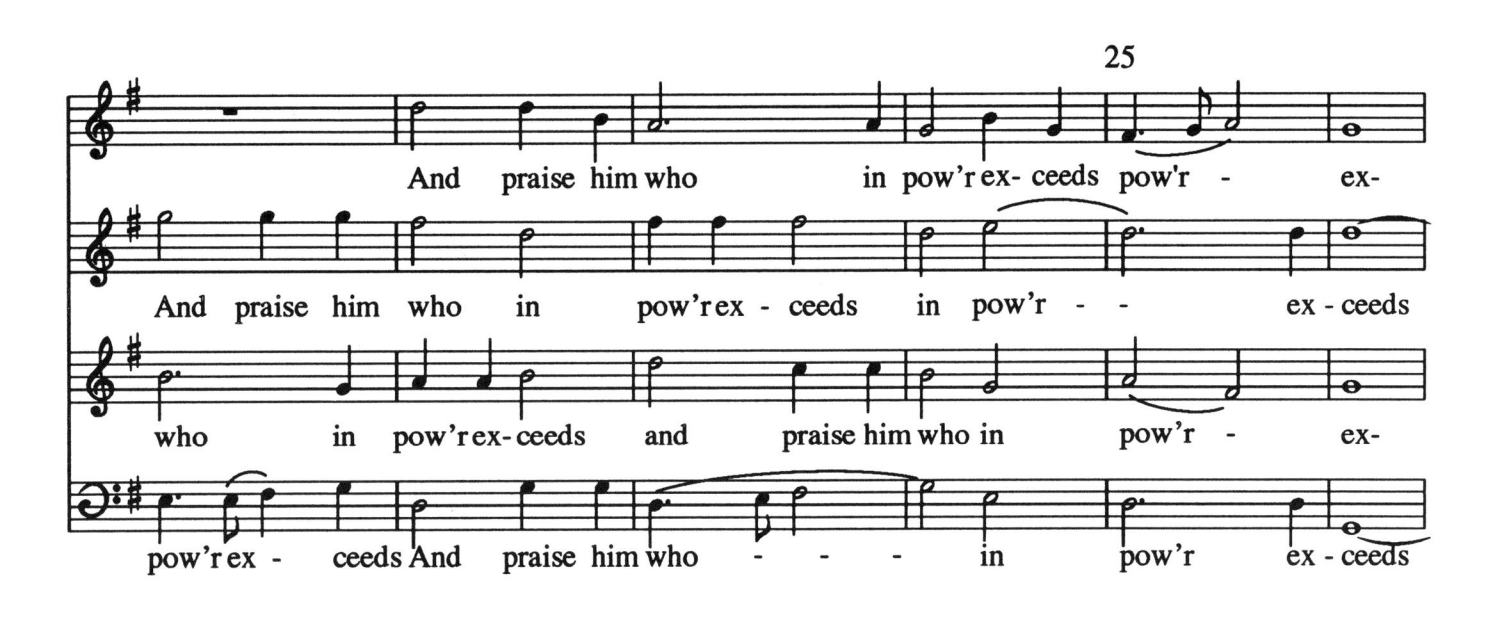

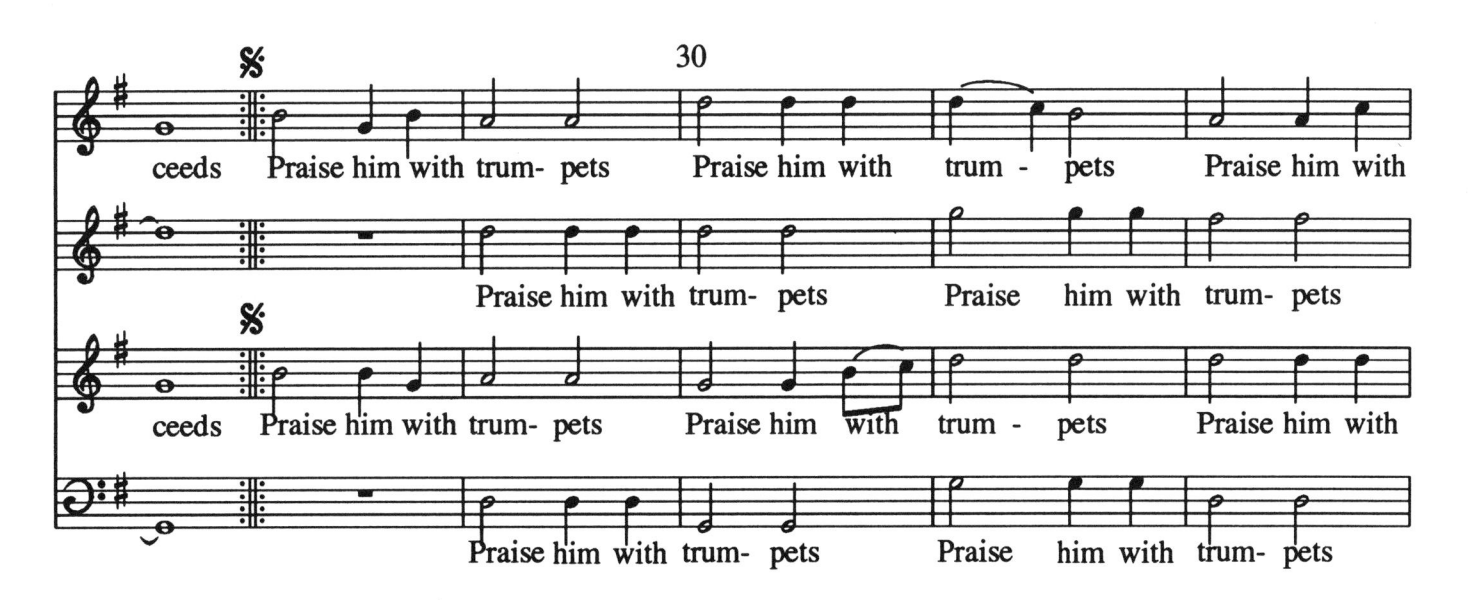

*Transcription © Edwin Macadam & Tony Singleton, 1995*

## 32            The Singing Seat

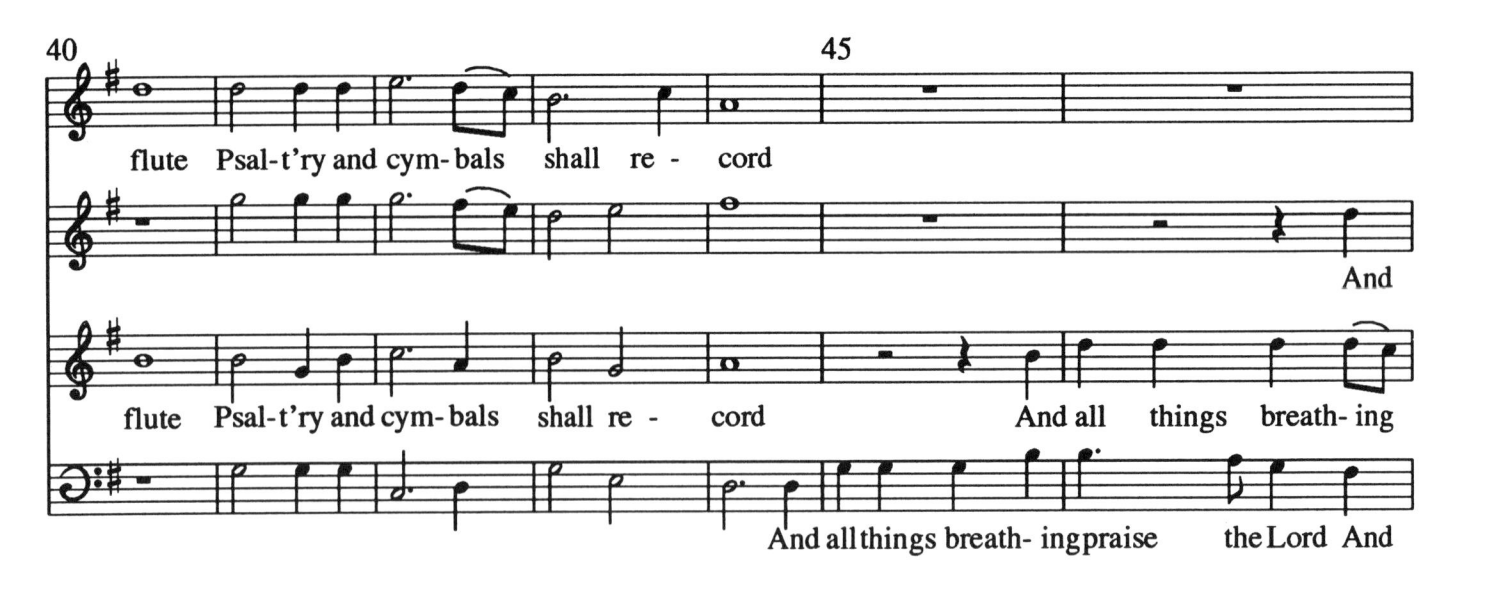

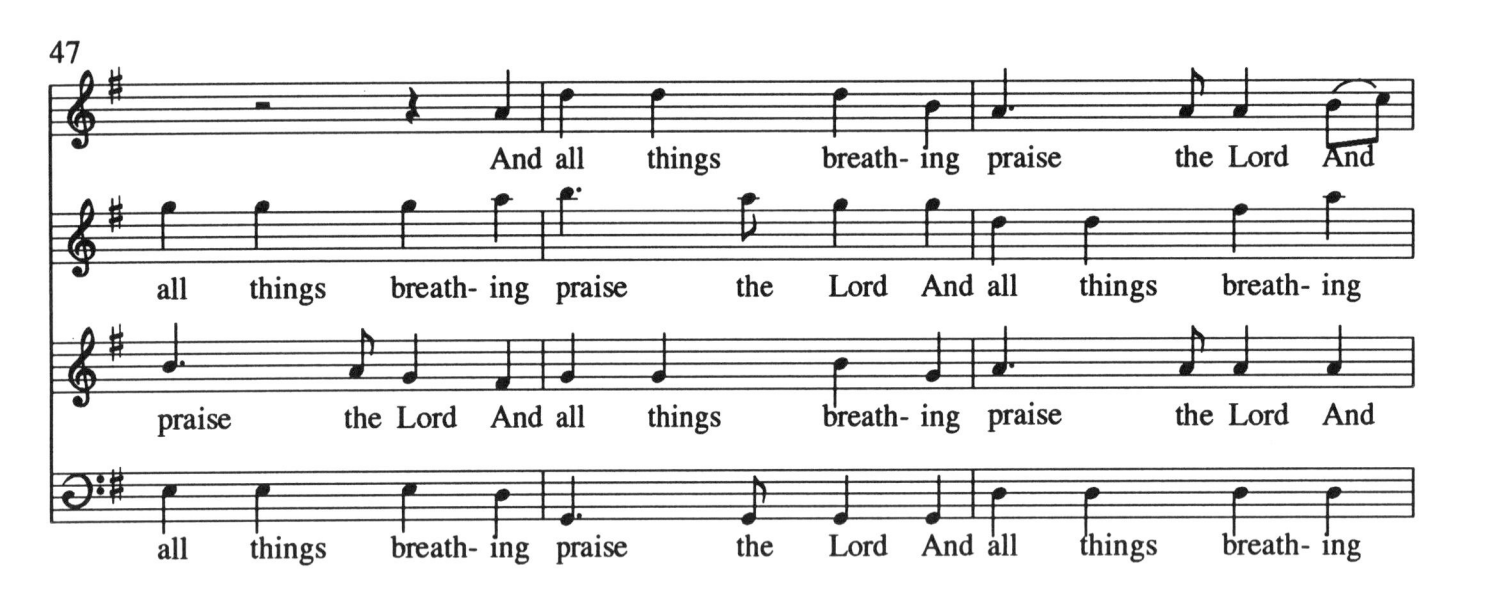

flute Psal-t'ry and cym-bals shall re - cord

And

flute Psal-t'ry and cym-bals shall re - cord And all things breath-ing

And all things breath-ing praise the Lord And

And all things breath-ing praise the Lord And

all things breath-ing praise the Lord And all things breath-ing

praise the Lord And all things breath-ing praise the Lord And

all things breath-ing praise the Lord And all things breath-ing

all things breath-ing all things breath-ing all things breath-ing prai - - se the Lord

praise the Lord And

all things breath-ing all things breath-ing all things breath-ing prai - - se the Lord

praise the Lord And

Transcription © Edwin Macadam & Tony Singleton, 1995

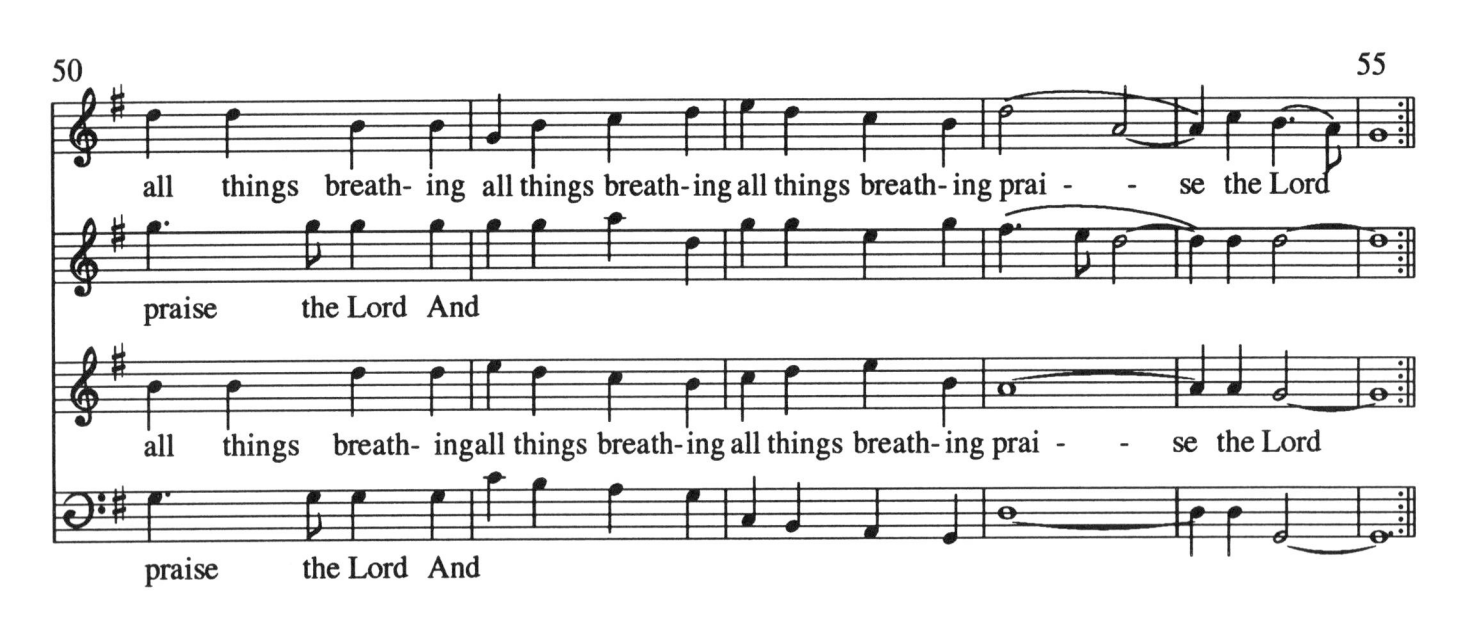

# *Glory Part to the 150 Hymn*

60
Hal-le- lu- jah Hal-le- lu- jah Hal-le- lu- jah Praise the Lord Hal-le- lu- jah Praise the Lord
Hal - le - lu - jah
Hal-le- lu- jah Hal-le- lu- jah Hal-le- lu- jah Praise the Lord Hal-le- lu- jah Praise the Lord
Hal - le - lu - jah

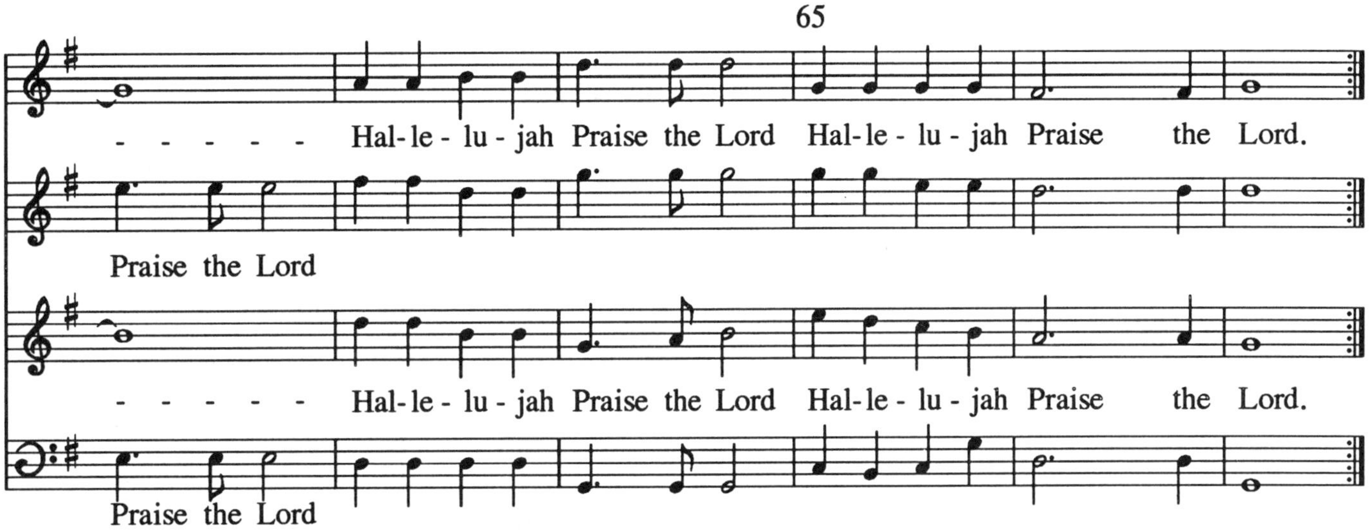
65
- - - - - Hal- le - lu - jah Praise the Lord Hal- le - lu - jah Praise the Lord.
Praise the Lord
- - - - - Hal- le - lu - jah Praise the Lord Hal- le - lu - jah Praise the Lord.
Praise the Lord

So far we have been unable to identify the composer of this short anthem. Unfortunately for us, the joyful and celebratory words have invited numerous composers in the West Gallery period to set them to music and a great many versions appear in printed sources.

Source: Acc. 19927 p 39

B.Hanson.

Door label of Catsfield Church

Transcription © Edwin Macadam & Tony Singleton, 1995

# The Dying Christian to his Soul

Voices: sTb

Vi-tal spark of heav'n-ly flame Quit O quit this mor-tal frame Trem-bling, ho-ping, ling'-ring, fly-ing, O the pain, the bliss of dy-ing. Cease fond na-ture, cease thy strife and let me lan-guish in-to life.

*Tenderly*

Hark! Hark! They whi-sper An-gels say They whi-sper An-gels say Hark! they whi-sper An-gels say

Transcription © Edwin Macadam & Tony Singleton, 1995

Si - ster spi - rit come a - way. Si - ster spi - rit come a - way. What is this ab - sorbs me
Si - ster spi - rit come a - way. What is this ab - sorbs me
quite, steals my sen - ses, shuts my sight, Drowns my spi - rit, draws my breath, Tell me my
quite, steals my sen - ses, shuts my sight, Drowns my spi - rit, draws my breath, Tell me my
soul can this be death? Tell me my soul can this be death? This world re - cedes, it
soul can this be death? Tell me my soul can this be death? This world re - cedes, it
di - sap - pears, Heav'n o - pens on my eyes, my ears, with sounds se - raph - ic
di - sap - pears, Heav'n o - pens on my eyes, my ears, with sounds se - raph - ic

65
With Spirit
ring Lend, lend your wings, I mount, I fly. O grave where is thy vic- to- ry? O
ring Lend, lend your wings, I mount, I fly. O grave where is thy vic- to- ry? O
70
grave where is thy vic- to- ry? O death where is thy sting? O grave where is thy vic- to- ry? O
grave where is thy vic- to- ry? O death where is thy sting? O grave where is thy vic- to- ry? O
cresc
p
75
death where is thy sting? Lend, lend your wings, I mount, I fly. O grave where is thy
death where is thy sting? Lend, lend your wings, I mount, I fly. O grave where is thy
cresc
p
*
cresc
f
vic- to- ry? thy vic- to- ry? O grave where is thy vic- to- ry? thy vic- to- ry? O death where is thy sting? O
vic- to- ry? thy vic- to- ry? O grave where is thy vic- to- ry? thy vic- to- ry? O death where is thy sting? O
cresc
f

The text is often referred to as 'Pope's Ode' and is reputed to be based on the words spoken by the Emperor Hadrian on his death-bed, transcripts of which appeared in a letter by Addison to the *Spectator* in 1711. It was subsequently published in various editions of Alexander Pope's *Works*, and from thence, taken for use in hymnals of the time. Many settings of the words were published and it is found in many ms collections. This version is almost identical to that by Edward Harwood, published in his *A Set of Hymn & Psalm Tunes* in 1786. Many reforming victorian clergy considered it irreverent and tried to prevent its performance, but the mourners often remained after the funeral service and sang it at the graveside in the incumbent's absence.

Sources:
Acc. 19927 p 56 (three part setting)
Acc. 19694 p 45 (four part setting)

In the 3 part ms setting, every section between double bars is marked with repeat dots. However, in the four part ms setting only bars 13 to 34 inc. are repeated (as above), which corresponds to Harwood's original composition.

Transcription © Edwin Macadam & Tony Singleton, 1995

# The Collect for the Seventh Sunday after Trinity

Voices: saTb

Lord of all power and might Lord of all power and might

Lord of all power and might Lord of all power and might Thou that art the giver

Thou that art the author of all good things

Thou that art the author

Graft in our hearts the love of Thy name the love of Thy name

Graft in our hearts the love of Thy name the love of Thy name In-crease in us true re-

Transcription © Edwin Macadam & Tony Singleton, 1995

# The Singing Seat

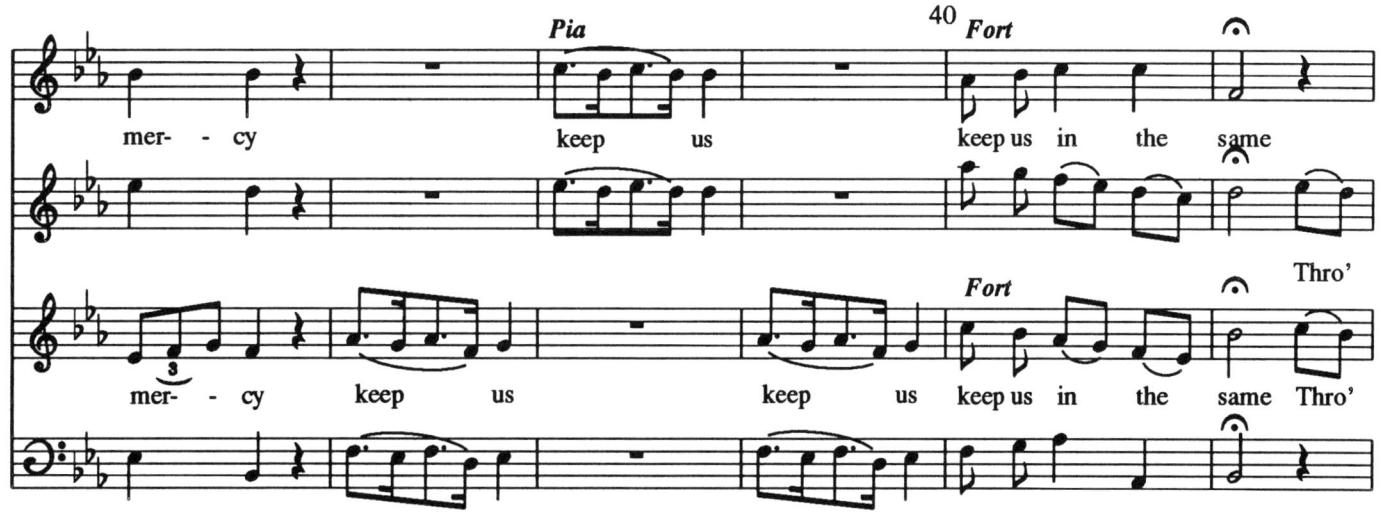

39

Transcription © Edwin Macadam & Tony Singleton, 1995

[Musical notation: four-part vocal score with text "Thro' Jesus Christ our Lord A-men A-men" / "Jesus Christ our Lord" / "Jesus Christ our Lord Thro' Jesus Christ our Lord A-men A-men", marked *Pia* at measure 45]

The piece appears as a three-part setting in a ms book from Beckley, only a few miles from Catsfield but little is known of the composer. In a printed music book in my possession (TS) it is set as a treble tune with organ accompaniment and ascribed to 'Mason' - the book has been rebound without its cover or title page!

In 1922, Herbert Blackman wrote to Canon MacDermott about his father and remarked that "in his later years, when, sometimes of a Sunday evening, he, my brother and I would sing some of these old tunes. My father did not need the book as he remembered the tunes and the words also, as I have no doubt many others of his class did." Alfred, an older bother, also wrote: "Born in 1849, I have seen some of the old veterans meet at my father's house, and have a few times heard them sing. The Collect for the 7th Sunday after Trinity as an anthem was a favourite. Although I never heard them sing in church, I have heard many times of what they used to do." It is a pity that Canon MacDermott didn't press him to commit more details to paper.

Sources: Acc. 19693 p 79 and 19694 p 40

Piscina in Catsfield church

Transcription © Edwin Macadam & Tony Singleton, 1995

# An Anthem taken from the 52nd Chapter of Isaiah

*The Singing Seat* — 41

Voices: saTb

Transcription © Edwin Macadam & Tony Singleton, 1995

# The Singing Seat

**Solo**

Loose thy-self from the bands the bands of thy neck Loo- - se thy self from the bands the bands of thy neck O cap- tive dau - ghter of Si - on

**Chorus**

Shake thy - self from the dust shake thy - self from the dust O Je - ru - sa - lem thou Ho - ly Ho - ly Ci - ty

Shake thy - self from the dust shake thy - self from the dust O Je - ru - sa - lem thou Ho - ly Ho - ly Ci - ty

Transcription © Edwin Macadam & Tony Singleton, 1995

## The Singing Seat

**Duet**

*How beau-ti-ful a-mong the mountains How beau-ti-ful a-mong the mountains How beau-ti-ful a-mong the*

*that brings glad ti-dings*
*moun-tains are the feet of him that brings glad ti-dings*

*of peace and sal-va-tion that saith un-to Si-on thy God reig-neth*

**Chorus**

Sing O heav'ns Sing O heav'ns Sing O heav'ns and be joy-ful O earth Sing O

Sing O hea —

Sing O heav'ns Sing O heav'ns Sing O heav'ns and be joy-ful O earth Sing O

*Play*

Transcription © Edwin Macadam & Tony Singleton, 1995

55
60
heav'ns Sing O heav'ns and be joy-ful O earth Break forth in- to joy Break forth in- to
hea- - - - -v'ns
heav'ns Sing O heav'ns and be joy-ful O earth Break forth in- to joy Hal-le - lu- jah Break forth in- to
Play
65
joy Sing to - ge- ther Sing to - ge- ther ye waste pla- ces of Je - ru- sa- lem
Hal - le - lu - jah
joy Sing to - ge- ther Sing to - ge- ther ye waste pla- ces of Je - ru- sa- lem
Ha-le - lu - jah
Play
70
Sing to - ge- ther Sing to - ge- ther ye waste pla- ces of Je - ru- sa - lem Hal- le - lu - jah For the Lord hath
Sing to - ge- ther Sing to - ge- ther ye waste pla- ces of Je - ru- sa - lem Hal- le - lu - jah For the Lord hath
Play

This anthem, written by W H Burgess of Heckfield in the northeast corner of Hampshire became very popular across the south of England. Little is known of the composer and there appear to be few other works ascribed to him.

Sources: Acc. 19693 p 56 and 19694 p 42
bar 14: denoted as Duet in ms.
* bar 16: in the top line the three quavers were written as a triplet and the bass quavers were unclear.
bars 37/8: the beams are editorial.

Transcription © Edwin Macadam & Tony Singleton, 1995

# Evening Hymn

Voices: saTb

As Bishop Ken's "Evening Hymn" was printed at the back of the Book of Common Prayer with the metrical psalms, it is not surprising that there are several settings in the Catsfield ms books, all based on Thomas Tallis's canon. The first four verses are written out in all cases, with slight differences from the Book of Common Prayer, from whence verse 5 has been added for completeness.

Transcription © Edwin Macadam & Tony Singleton, 1995

The Singing Seat

(1)
Glory to Thee, my God, this night,
    For all the blessings of the light;
Keep me, O keep me, King of Kings,
    Under thy own Almighty wings.

(2)
Forgive me, Lord, for thy dear Son,
    The ill that I this day have done;
That, with the world, myself, and Thee,
    I, ere I sleep, at peace may be.

(3)
Teach me to live, that I may dread
    The grave as little as my bed;
Teach me to die, that so I may
    With joy behold the judgement day.

(4)
O let my soul on Thee repose
    And with sweet sleep mine eyelids close;
Sleep that may me more active make,
    To serve my God when I awake.

(5)
If in the night I sleepless lie,
    My soul with heav'nly thoughts supply;
Let no ill dreams disturb my rest,
    No powers of darkness me molest.

(6)
Praise God from whom all blessings flow;
    Praise Him, all creatures here below;
Praise Him above, angelic host,
    Praise Father, Son, and Holy Ghost.

Sources: Acc. 19693 p 14 - has symphony and verses 1 - 4 and doxology, essentially this transcription.
    Acc. 19926 p 30 has no symphony and only verses 1 - 4; alto and tenor parts are in the alto clef.
    Acc. 19927 p 17 has no symphony and verses 1 - 4 and doxology; all parts are in the alto clef!
* bar 4: A in ms; bar7: A in ms; bar12: C in ms; bar14: C in ms; bar15: C in ms; bar 32: D in ms.

Transcription © Edwin Macadam & Tony Singleton, 1995

# Morning Hymn

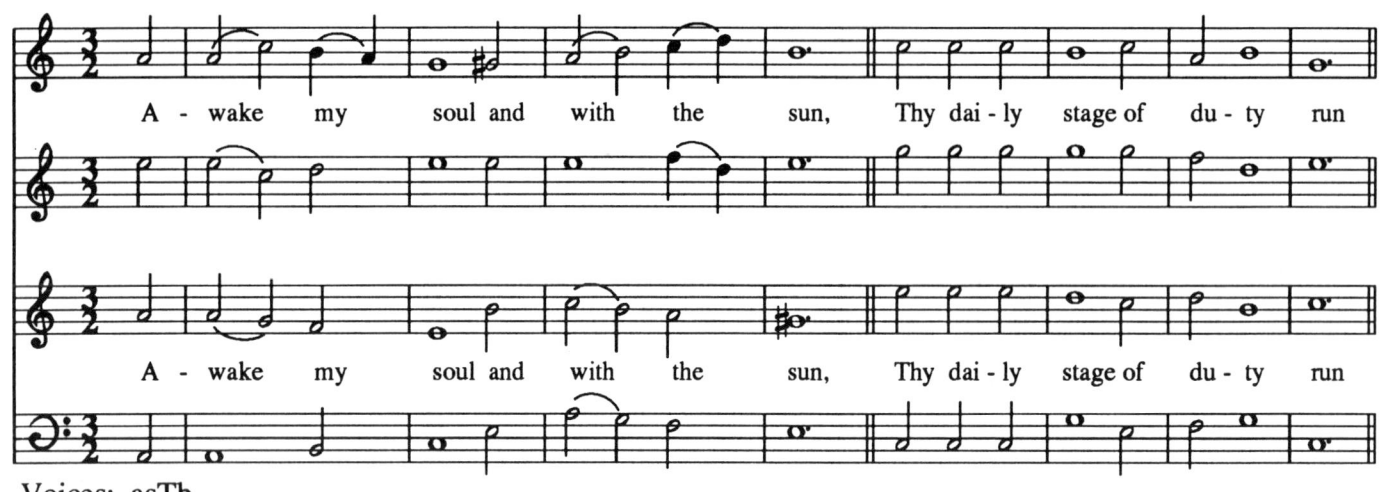

Voices: asTb

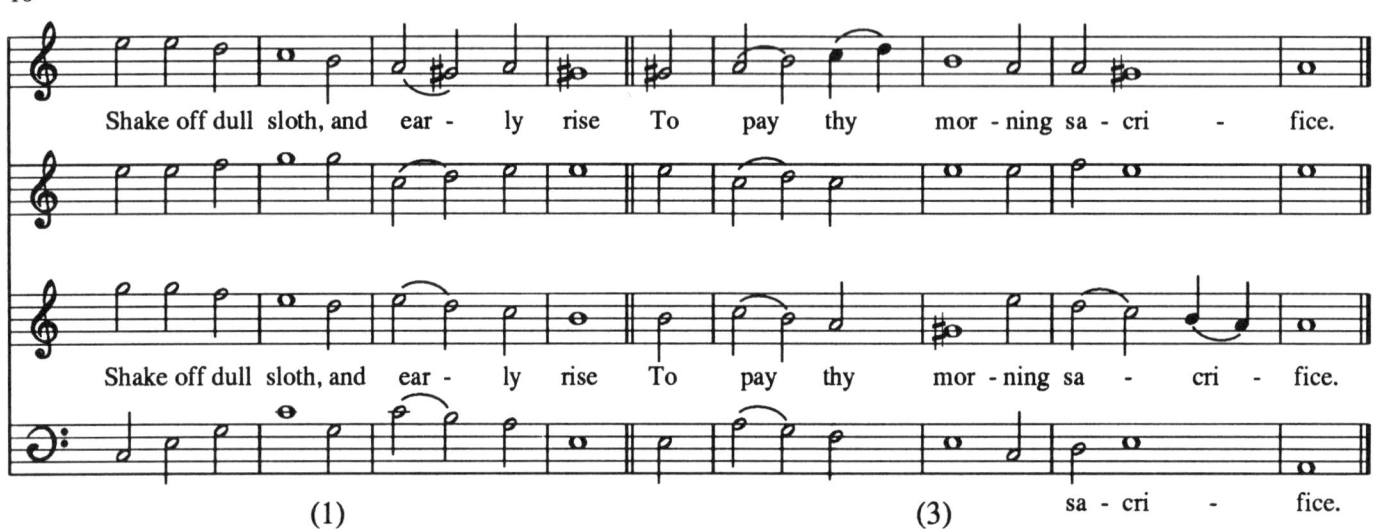

(1)
Awake my soul and with the sun.
　Thy daily stage of duty run.
Shake off dull sloth and early rise
　To pay thy morning sacrifice.

(2)
Glory to Thee who safe hast kept,
　And hast refresh'd me whilst I slept,
Grant, Lord, when I from death shall wake,
　I may of endless life partake.

(3)
Lord, I my vows to Thee renew,
　Scatter my sins as morning dew.
Guard my first spring of thought and will
　And with Thyself my spirit fill.

(4)
Direct, control, suggest, this day
　All I design, or do, or say,
That all my powers, with all my might
　In Thy sole glory may unite.

**Doxolgy**
Praise God, from whom all blessings flow
　Praise Him, all creatures here below,
　Praise Him above angelic host,
　Praise Father, Son and Holy Ghost.

This is one of three different tunes for the Morning Hymn found in the Catsfield ms books. These words, written out with the music, are verses 1, 5, 6, 7 and 8 written by Bishop Ken in 1695. The music is Jeremiah Clark's setting of the *Evening Hymn* in Henry Playford's *Divine Companion*, published in 1701. Sources: Acc. 19927 p 16; Acc. 19926 p 0 (before page number 1!) has tenor/bass only as a two part setting.

Transcription © Edwin Macadam & Tony Singleton, 1995

# Belvidere CM Hymn

Blest be the dear u-ni-ting love That will not let us part That will not let us part. Our bo-dies may far off re-move Our bo-dies may far off re-move We still are one in heart We still are one in heart

Voices: asTb

(2)
Join'd in one spirit to our head
Where he appoints we go,
And still in Jesus' footsteps tread
And shew his praise below.

(3)
Partakers of the Saviour's grace,
The same in mind and heart,
Nor joy nor grief nor time nor place,
Nor life nor death can part.

(4)
But let us hasten to the day
Which shall our flesh restore,
When death shall all be done away
And bodies part no more.

Source: Acc. 19690-2 p 22

Transcription © Edwin Macadam & Tony Singleton, 1995

# Hymn 165 Dr Watts Book2

Voices: saTb

Long have I sat beneath the sound Of Thy salvation Lord Of Thy salvation Lord But still how weak my faith is found And knowledge of Thy word And knowledge of Thy word And knowledge of Thy word And knowledge of Thy word

Transcription © Edwin Macadam & Tony Singleton, 1995

# The Singing Seat

(1)
Long have I sat beneath the sound
　Of thy salvation, Lord
But still how weak my faith is found
　And knowledge of thy word.

(2)
Oft I frequent thy holy place
　And hear almost in vain
How small a portion of thy grace
　My mem'ry can retain.

(5)
Great God, thy sov'reign pow'r impart
　To give thy word success
Write thy salvation in my heart
　And make me learn thy grace.

(6)
Shew my forgetful feet the way.
　That leads to joys on high.
There knowledge grows without decay
　And love shall never die.

This hymn, written by Isaac Watts, was originally entitled "Unfruitfulness lamented" in *Horae Lyricae*, published between 1706 and 1709. It is no. 665 in *Wesley's Hymns* where it is described as a "Prayer for Quickening Grace", but there the verses appear as follows:

(1)
Long have I sat beneath the sound
　Of thy salvation, Lord;
But still how weak my faith is found,
　And knowledge of thy word!

(2)
My gracious Saviour and my God
　How little art thou known
By all the judgements of thy rod,
　Or blessings of thy throne!

(3)
How cold and feeble is my love!
　How negligent my fear!
How low my hope of joys above!
　How few affections there!

(4)
Great God, thy sovereign aid impart,
　To give thy word success;
Write thy salvation on my heart
　And make me learn thy grace.

(5)
Show my forgetful feet the way
　That leads to joys on high,
Where knowledge grows without decay,
　And love shall never die.

Source: Acc. 19927 p 14

Transcription © Edwin Macadam & Tony Singleton, 1995

# Hymn 428 Rippon
## Tune: Calcutta

O'er the gloo-my hills of dark-ness Look my soul be still and gaze All the pro-mi-ses do tra-vail with a glo- - - rious day of grace.

Voices: saTb

Bles-sed jub'lee Bles-sed jub'lee Let Thy glorious morning dawn

*Instr*

Let Thy glo-rious mor-ning dawn Let Thy glo-rious mor-ning dawn Let Thy glo- - - rious mor-ning dawn Let Thy

Transcription © Edwin Macadam & Tony Singleton, 1995

# The Singing Seat

(1)
O'er the gloomy hills of darkness
    Look my soul, be still and gaze
All the promises do travail
    With a glorious day of grace
Blessed Jub'lee, blessed Jub'lee
    Let thy glorious morning dawn.

(2)
Let the Indian, let the Negro
    Let the rude barbarian see
That divine and blessed conquest
    Once obtain'd on Calvary
Let the gospel, let the gospel
    Loud resound from pole to pole.

(3)
May the glorious day approaching
    Thine eternal love proclaim
And the everlasting gospel
    Spread abroad the Holy name.
O'er the borders, o'er the borders
    Of the great Immanuel's land.

The tune, Calcutta, was one of Thomas Clark's earliest and most popular compositions, being published in his *First Book of Psalm and Hymn Tunes* in 1805. It also appeared later in The Union Tune Book, edited by Clark. The text by W Williams of Pantycelyn, Wales, was first published in Welsh in his *Gloria in Excelsis: or Hymns of Praise to God the Lamb* in 1772 as "Dros y beynian tywyll niwliog". It was republished in English with amendments in Rippon's *Baptist Selection* as no. 428 and became famous in the missionary fields where it was translated into many other languages. In these days of political correctness it may be considered inappropriate to sing the words of verse 2 above so the following verses are given as additions and alternatives.

Kingdoms wild that sit in darkness
    Let them have the glorious light
And from eastern coast to western
    May the morning chase the night
And redemption, and redemption
    Freely purchased win the day.

Fly abroad, eternal gospel
    Win and conquer, never cease
May thy lasting wide dominions
    Multiply and still increase
May thy sceptre, may thy sceptre
    Sway th'enlightened world around.

Sources: Acc. 19690-2 p 2, 19927 p 7 and 19693 p 70. In the last two ms books, the crotchets in the last two bars above are written as minims (in four bars), thus doubling the length of the last repeat of "Let Thy glorious morning dawn". They also lack the instrumental bar in the bass at bar 10. In acc. 19693, the top two vocal lines are exchanged.

Transcription © Edwin Macadam & Tony Singleton, 1995

# Jubilee Hymn

*The Singing Seat*

Blow ye the trum- -pet blow The glad-ly so-lemn sound Let all the na-tions know To earth's re-mo-test bound The year of ju-bi-lee The year of ju-bi-lee is come The year of ju-bi-lee is come Re-turn ye ran-som'd Re-turn ye ran- - -som'd sin-ners home.

Voices: saTb

(2)
Jesus our great High Priest
Hath full atonement made
Ye weary Spirits rest
Ye mournful soul be glad
*The year of Jubilee, etc*

(3)
Extol the Lamb of God
The all-atoning Lamb
Redemption in his blood
Throughout the world proclaim
*The year of Jubilee, etc*

(4)
The gospel trumpet hear
The news of heav'nly grace
And sav'd from earth appear
Before your Saviour's face.
*The year of Jubilee, etc*

Source: Acc. 19927 p 5 (although at present it is stuck into acc. 19926)   * bar 11: the sharp has been added.

Transcription © Edwin Macadam & Tony Singleton, 1995

# Advent Hymn

*Lo he comes with clouds descending Once for favoured sinners slain*
*Lo he comes with clouds descending Once for favoured sinners slain*

*Thousand thousand saints attending Swell the triumph of his train*
*Thousand thousand saints attending Swell the triumph of his train*

*Hallelujah! Hallelujah! God appears on earth to reign*
*Hallelujah! Hallelujah! God appears on earth to reign*

(2)
Every eye shall now behold him
Rob'd in dreadful majesty
Those who set at nought and sold him
Pierc'd and nailed him to the tree
Deeply wailing (x2)
Shall the true Messiah see.

(3)
The dear tokens of his Passion
Still his dazzling body bears
Cause of endless exultation
To his ransom'd worshippers
With what rapture (x2)
Gaze we on those glorious scars.

(4)
Yea, Amen, let all adore Thee
High on Thy eternal throne
Saviour, take the pow'r and glory
Claim the kingdom for Thine
Hallelujah! (x2)        [own
Everlasting God! come down.

Source: Acc. 19690 p 34          This is no. 66 in *Wesley's Hymns* with minor differences.

Transcription © Edwin Macadam & Tony Singleton, 1995

# Nativity

Voices: asTb

Hark Hark the her-ald an-gels sing Glo-ry to the new-born king
Peace on earth and mer-cy mild God and sin-ners re-con-cil'd!
Joy-ful all ye na-tions rise Join the tri-umph of the skies

*Instr* *Voices*

This popular modern carol has evolved from verses by Charles Wesley, published in his *Hymns & Sacred Poems* (1739), as "Hark how all the welkin rings, Glory to the Kings of Kings." The text was revised in 1743 and forms the basis of that added to the Book of Common Prayer in 1782. Charles Burney (1726-1814) was a composer, musical historian and critic, organist, traveller and diarist and three pages are devoted to him in the Dictionary of National Biography.

Source: Acc. 19694 p 38

Transcription © Edwin Macadam & Tony Singleton, 1995

(1)
Hark the herald angels sing,
    Glory to the new-born king.
Peace on earth and mercy mild,
    God and sinners reconcil'd!
Joyful all ye nations rise,
    Join the triumph of the skies.
With th'angelic host proclaim,
    Christ is born in Bethlehem.
    *Hark the herald angels sing*
    *Glory to the new-born King!*

(2)
Christ by highest heav'n ador'd,
    Christ the everlasting Lord,
Late in time behold him come,
    Offspring of virgin's womb:
Veil'd in flesh the Godhead he,
    Hail th'incarnate Deity;
Pleas'd as man with man appear,
    Jesus our Immanuel here.

(3)
Hail the heav'n-born Prince of Peace!
    Hail the Son of righteousness!
Light and life to all he brings,
    Ris'n with healing in his wings.
Mild he lays his Glory by,
    Born that man no more may die;
Born to raise the sons of earth,
    Born to give them second birth.

Transcription © Edwin Macadam & Tony Singleton, 1995

# A Hymn for Christmas Day

Voices: asTb

Christians awake, arise, rejoice and sing Behold glad tidings unto you I bring. A child is born his wonders will increase his wonders will increase The everlasting father, Prince of Peace.

Transcription © Edwin Macadam & Tony Singleton, 1995

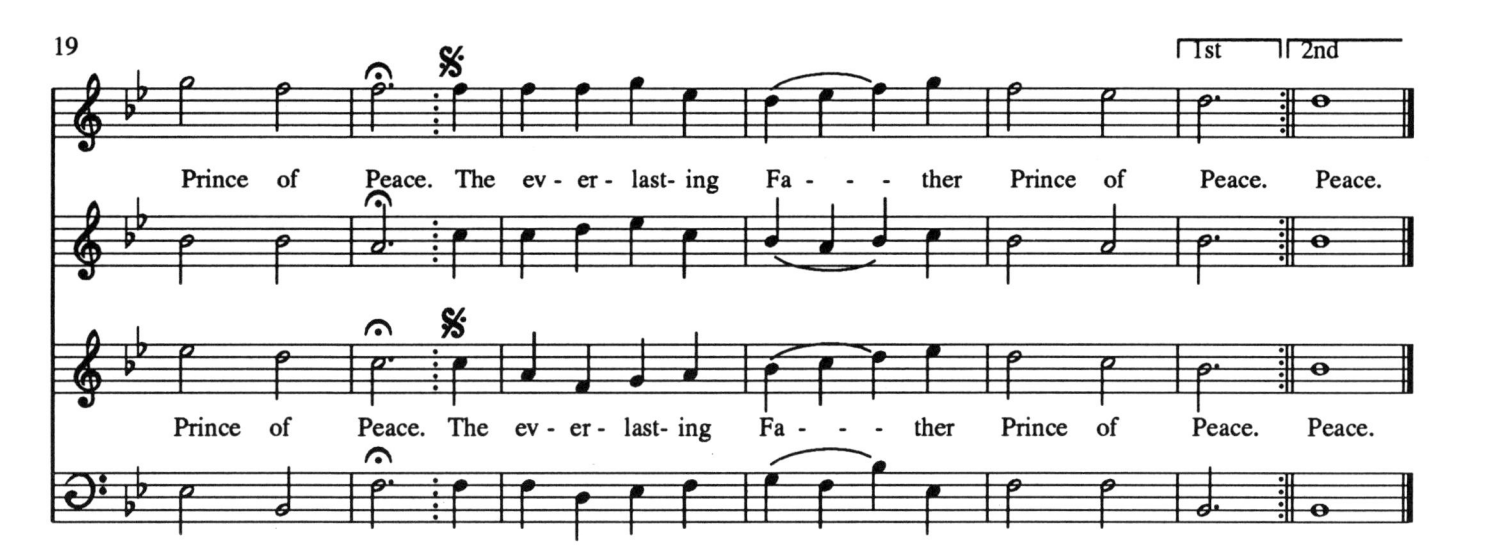

### (1)
Christians awake, arise, rejoice and sing
  Behold glad tidings unto you I bring.
A child is born, His wonders will increase
  The everlasting father, Prince of Peace.

### (2)
Sweet Jesus Christ, our saviour as we find
  From sin, He is redeemer of mankind
Now reigns in heaven above the stormy sky
  Where saints and angels sing eternally.

### (3)
This princely child was born of David's line
  His name is wonderful of great divine
Rejoice, rejoice with hymns of joy and mirth
  And worship Him all nations upon earth.

### (4)
Let earth and heav'n in joyful accents ring
  In praises to our great almighty King
Let every mortal catch the happy sound
  Where peace and happiness on earth abound.

The piece does not seem to have survived into the twentieth century, although "Christians arise, salute the happy morn" by J Byrom, more popular in Kent, has done so and appears in *Hymns Ancient and Modern* and *The Methodist Church Hymnal*.

Source: Acc. 19926 p 52 (source of this version) and 19927 p 48 where the soprano and alto lines are exchanged, ie saTb assignment of voices. In the ms books, the music is repeated from the start of the duet (bar 9) but this is inconsistent with the first and second time bars at the end. Consequently, the repeat has been amended as above. * bar 18: the rests have been added.

Transcription © Edwin Macadam & Tony Singleton, 1995

# A Funeral Hymn (1)

Voices: saTb

Transcription © Edwin Macadam & Tony Singleton, 1995

(1)
My life's a shade, my days
    Apace to death decline.
My Lord is life, he'll raise
    My dust again, e'en mine.
*Chorus:*
    *Sweet truth to me, I shall arise*
    *And with these eyes my Saviour see.*

(2)
My peaceful grave shall keep
    My bones till the sweet day
I wake from my long sleep
    And leave my bed of clay.
*Chorus:*

(3)
My Lord his angels shall
    Their golden trumpets sound
At whose most welcome call
    My grave shall be unbound.
*Chorus:*

(4)
I said, sometimes with tears.
    Ah me, I'm loth to die.
Lord, silence thou those fears,
    My life's with thee on high.
*Chorus:*

(5)
What means my trembling heart
    To be thus shy of death?
My life and I shan't part
    Though I resign my breath.
*Chorus:*

(6)
Then welcome harmless grave,
    By thee to heav'n I'll go.
My Lord his death shall save
    Me from the flames below.
*Chorus:*
    *Sweet truth to me, I shall arise*
    *And with these eyes my Saviour see.*

This is a setting by William Knapp (1698/9 - 1768), parish clerk of Poole in Dorset, of a hymn entitled "Resurrection" by Samuel Crossman (c.1624 - 1683), Prebendary and later Dean of Bristol Cathedral, based on Job 19, v25 and published in 1664 in a pamphlet entitled *The Young Man's Meditation, or Some few Sacred Poems upon Select Subjects, and Scriptures*. The musical setting is almost identical to the version found in the 5th edition of Knapp's *New Church Melody, being a set of Anthems, Psalms, Hymns, etc, on various occasions, in Four Parts, with a great variety of other Anthems, Psalm , Hymns, etc, composed after a Method entirely new, and never printed before*. Even the alto part in the Catsfield manuscript book is written out in the alto clef, just as in the original, but has been transcribed here for ease of performance.

Source: Acc. 19926 p 84

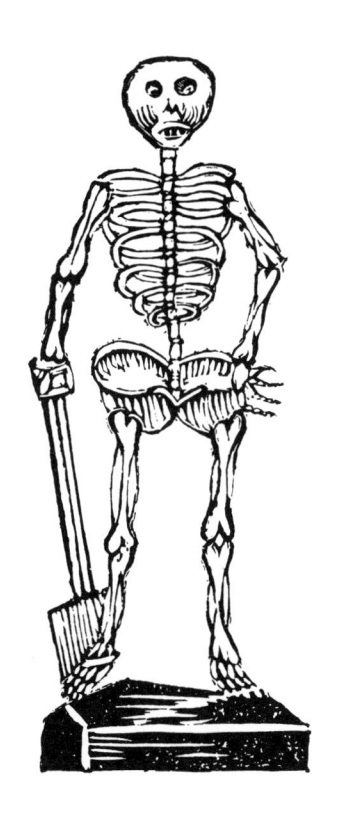

Transcription © Edwin Macadam & Tony Singleton, 1995

# A Funeral Hymn (2)

Into this world we nothing brought Nor nothing can retain

Voices: sTb

But as from dust we first were wrought To dust must turn again

(1)
Into this world we nothing brought
    Nor nothing can retain
But as from dust we first were wrought
    To dust must turn again

(2)
Our life's a journey full of care
    No wealth from death can save:
Each step we take more near we are
    To our dark silent grave.

(3)
It is not only death we dread
    But rather what's behind,
For though we in the grave are laid
    We sure shall judgement find.

(4)
Arise you dead to judgement come
    This sound we all must hear.
How will the wicked dread their doom
    And quake for guilt and fear.

(5)
Whilst godly men of heav'n possess'd
    Lift up their heads with joy
Absolved and blest with Christ in rest
    To all eternity.

(6)
To Father, Son and Holy Ghost
    The undivided three,
To the soul giver of all life
    Glory for ever be.

This piece first appeared in print in 1767 in *The Elements of Musick made Easy; or an Universal Introduction to the Whole Art of Musick, Book III*, by William Tans'ur, senior, who styled himself "Musico-Theorico".

Source: Acc. 19690-2 p 15

Transcription © Edwin Macadam & Tony Singleton, 1995